BRIEFLY KNOCKED UNCONSCIOUS BY A
LOW-FLYING DUCK

STORIES FROM 2ND STORY

ELEPHANT
ROCK
BOOKS

Thanks to the Generous Support of the Leo and Rose Burrello Literary Endowment.

For information about permission to reproduce sections from this book, contact Permissions at elephantrockbooks@gmail.com. Elephant Rock Books are distributed by Small Press United, a division of Independent Publishers Group.

In several instances, names have been changed to protect privacy.

ISBN: 978-0-9846700-6-2

Library of Congress Control Number: 2012940972

Printed in the United States of America

Book Design by Amanda Schwarz

First Edition
10 9 8 7 6 5 4 3 2 1

Elephant Rock Books
Ashford, CT

Essays in this anthology have previously appeared, in somewhat different forms, in the following publications: "This Teacher Talks Too Fast" in *Everyone Remain Calm*; "Amber" in *Annalemma*; "CoverGirl" in *INTHEFRAY*; and "Running on Empty" in *Fresh Yarn*. Additionally, many of these essays appeared in *Cell Stories*, a literary journal for mobile devices.

This book is for our amazing audience, who has been attending our performances for over a decade.

Welcome to our pages.

CONTENTS

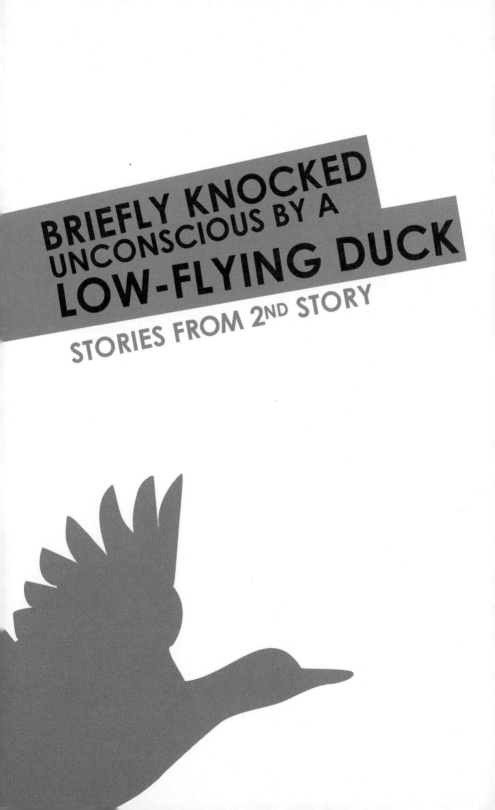

BRIEFLY KNOCKED UNCONSCIOUS BY A LOW-FLYING DUCK

STORIES FROM 2ND STORY

ON THE POWER OF STORYTELLING
(OR, WHY WE DO WHAT WE DO THE WAY WE DO IT)

The second floor of Webster's Wine Bar in Chicago is packed—people are lined up along the walls of the rectangular room, squashed into leather banquettes, crowded into chairs and sofas. The air is hazy with summer-is-coming humidity, and tonight's performance is about to begin. "Welcome to 2nd Story!" says our host for the evening, and the audience cheers. "We have three stories for you tonight, and we'll space them out through the evening like courses—a ten-minute story, then a ten-minute break for you to talk to your friends (or make new friends), maybe grab a drink or step outside for a smoke, and then we'll have the next story. We'll lather, rinse, and repeat this three times over the course of the evening, and voila! World saved!" The audience laughs, but we *really mean it* when we say that.

The host explains our name: "We tell the first story in the hope that you, our audience, will then tell each other *your* stories—that's what we mean by 2nd Story." Heads nod—I observe shared glances, glances that say, *Wow, they're talking about me. I'm important to how this event runs*—and then the first storyteller is introduced. "Ladies and Gentlemen, please welcome Khanisha Foster!" She's at the far end of the room, opposite from where I'm standing, and as the lights come up on her, a stillness settles over the room. She begins her story, "The Kids and the King," and then I watch the audience. This is one of my favorite things to do as the Artistic Director of 2nd Story. Wherever the performance—at a theater, a conference, a literary festival, a storytelling night for families, or here on the second floor of Webster's Wine Bar—I always stand at the back of the room so I can see the audience.

The audience is the reason why we do what we do the way we do it. Our prioritization of audience is what makes 2nd Story different from other reading or storytelling events. We focus on personal narrative (many people do that), but our mission isn't to tell great stories (which might seem odd, since our stories are so awesome). Our actual *Mission*[1] is to use stories to build community. It's not just about creating good stories; it's about employing those stories to connect people to one another. Ultimately, the experience of our audience is the most important thing we do, so while our stories must necessarily be good (we would not be prioritizing our audience if we told crappy stories), in order to truly bring people together, they must also be universal. I call this "audience-forward" thinking. This is why our story development process is so deeply collaborative, and why we depend so much on the outside eye[2] to help our tellers craft their stories.

The teller knows the story intimately—he or she lived it—so it's imperative that there's someone (or, preferably, many someones) who did *not* experience it who can and will give the teller feedback about what's working and what's not, what's missing and what's unclear, what questions linger and what the story is about. To a certain extent, it doesn't matter what the opinion of the teller is—if

---

[1] The 2nd Story Mission: We believe that sharing stories has the power to educate, connect, and inspire. We exist to host the celebration and ritual of shared stories.

[2] The "outside eye" is 2nd Story-speak for all the different folks who work with a storyteller as he or she prepares for one of our events. This includes the other tellers for that evening, the curator, the director, the sound designer or musicians, and others.

your outside eye isn't hearing what you think is on the page, there's a disconnect in the writing. This is the gift of our process.

Khanisha finishes her story, the band segues into the opening bars of Sam Cooke's "A Change is Gonna Come," and the applause is deafening. She smiles, moves out of the chair, and makes her way back to me, beaming all the way. As she goes "off-stage" (really, to the dry goods area that hides just behind the wall against which I'm leaning), the audience erupts into conversation, telling their own stories. In a minute, she will re-emerge; I can already see people looking for her. Her story touched something in them, and now they want to share it with her.

This is why we tell our stories.

There is something transformative about sharing air with the person who Actually Had the Experience, something about being able to walk up to them afterwards, introduce yourself, and have a conversation about the story that you just heard. This connection (or community building between adults) between teller and audience creates an intimacy that reading, conventional theater, and our plugged-lives cannot and do not deliver.

It is mission-critical for us that an audience member is able to approach a storyteller after he or she has been in the chair[3] and say, "That happened to me, too," and for the teller to be able to engage in an honest conversation with them. That's part of the whole "bringing people together" thing. For years, this need was not clear to us, and a lot of what we told was fiction, or pretty darn close. But in the midst of that debate, one of our tellers, Deb R. Lewis, wrote and performed "Why I Hate Strawberries," a story about her grandfather sexually abusing her. We realized then that it would be a travesty of conscience if an audience member were to walk up to her afterwards and say, "That happened to me, too," and Deb were to reply, "Oh, well, I made that up." That story—and that realization—crystallized for me that if this were true for one story, it had to be true for all of our work. Since then, we've told only real stories.

---

[3] "In the chair" is 2nd Story Speak for performing a story at one of our events.

The host returns to introduce our second teller, "Ladies and gentlemen, what a wonderful night! I love walking through the room and hearing all of your stories! Let's keep it going—help me give a warm welcome to Kim Morris!" The audience applauds as Kim moves to the microphone and launches into "Super K."

That's the term we've settled on: *real*. We've had endless debates[4] about truth versus fiction in our stories—our culture is in a constant conversation about this issue, with case after case held up for public debate, artist after artist called to the carpet. I believe there are two clearly defined ends of the spectrum: nonfiction, anchored by journalism (where the contract with the audience is that the story is fact-based, balanced reporting) and fiction (where the contract with the audience is that this stuff is made up.) In between these two extremes is a super gray area where everything else resides: essays, personal narrative, creative nonfiction, memoir, fables, myth, even history, to a certain degree. So at 2nd Story we call our stories "real." Yes, they happened. Yes, we fact-checked them. Yes, sometimes dreams, or memories, or fantasies, or alternate realities come into play, because that's the nature of being human: we all replay reality in our heads, engage in fantasy lives that parallel what is actually happening in the world. In fact, that's what Kim is doing right now— as she tells the story of a bike race, she flips between three different threads: the scene of the race, a scene in the doctor's office, and imagining herself as a tiny superhero who can enter people's bodies. The audience is swept up in her flights of fantasy: who hasn't sat in traffic and imagined themselves suddenly able to push a button and make the car fly? Or been pushed around as a kid and imagined themselves suddenly victorious over the schoolyard bullies? Just because those scenarios are imagined doesn't mean they are any less *real*. Especially when faced with tragedy—things that just we can't

---

[4] I'm not kidding—we're talking about years of debate, where the writer-types in the group were all, "Yeah, but the use of fictional techniques allows us to craft the best story possible!" and the theater-types were all "But the contract with the audience is that these stories are true, that they actually happened! They can't be fictional." People, I'm telling you: It. Was. Heated.

wrap our minds around—we use our imaginations to help us cope.

Kim ends her story, and the audience is struck in the chest, floored by her defeat. The applause has a different tenor this time—it's just as strong, just as heartfelt, but there's a sense of the audience circling the wagons around her, honoring the vulnerability that she just shared, promising to protect her. I give Kim's arm a squeeze as she slips past me into the dry goods area, and she gives me a small smile, spent. All the people in the room have had the wind knocked out of them, and as the applause dies, there's a beat, then a breath as the room absorbs the fierce beauty of what she's just shared. One quiet moment, and then the roomful of stories start again, more earnest, subdued, and urgent than last time.

Yes, I think. *This is why we do what we do.*

A few minutes later, the host introduces our final teller of the night, Ric Walker, and he starts his story, "Push, Kick, Coast." In a half-hour or so, I will thank people as they pour out of the bar and into the spring night, but for now, I lean against the wall and, again, watch the audience watching the teller. A few of them, like Ric, probably spent a good amount of their youth in a roller rink, but everyone can remember the bluster and bravado of being a teenager. This universality is vital to the stories that we tell: the "what happens" (the plot, or sequence of actions) is going to be unique to each story and teller, but the *impact* of it, the "what it's about," is something that speaks to the human condition. We think about it like layers of an onion: the further you peel it back, the larger the piece that's performed, the more universal the story is.

With each layer, our storytellers dig deeper and deeper into the subtext of the tale they are telling, and this is where the artistry and craft come in. By employing the tools of creative writing (detail and dialogue and character and scene and narrative distance), the artist discovers not so much the plot (not the *truth*) of the story, because that is relatively immutable, but the *meaning*, the thing that this story is *about* for themselves—and for the audience. Everything that we do is in service to the story, and the story is in service to the mission of connecting people to each other by revealing a larger emotional truth.

The end of Ric's story is palpable. The words "push, kick, coast," fill the air one last time and the oxygen is sucked out of the room. The opening notes of Thelma Houston's "Don't Leave Me This Way" fill the room, and there's a moment of suspension as we process the experience that we just shared. Ric makes his way to the back of the room, riding the wave of applause that, as it dies out, transforms into eighty simultaneous conversations.

Mission accomplished.

Our hope is that this anthology will do something similar. That you, dear reader, will be moved, or challenged, or empowered by these stories; that you will share them, talk about them, and be inspired to tell your own stories because of them. After all, that's our mission.

Amanda Delheimer Dimond
Artistic Director, 2nd Story

BRIEFLY KNOCKED UNCONSCIOUS BY A LOW-FLYING DUCK

BY MATT MILLER

In the summer of 1998, I worked as trainer in the Wild Wings Bird Show at SeaWorld Ohio. It was a rainy, humid summer: the summer of *Saving Private Ryan* and *Armageddon*; the summer of "Tubthumping" by Chumbawumba, "I Don't Want To Miss A Thing" by Aerosmith, and definitely "Gettin' Jiggy Wit It" by Will Smith. It was the summer Phil Hartman was murdered by his wife. The summer I broke my ankle. And it was the summer I learned about cancer. But mostly, it was the summer I spent with the birds.

As far as northeast Ohio was concerned, SeaWorld was one of the best summer jobs around: decent money, lots of hot girls, and cool animals. Top five random SeaWorld Facts:

Fact #1: Most people don't know that SeaWorld Ohio was the first SeaWorld theme park in the Midwest, and that makes a lot of sense, as it's very difficult to go whale watching in northeast Ohio.

Fact #2: The vast majorities of the animals at SeaWorld were born in captivity or were seriously injured in the wild and rescued.

Fact #3: SeaWorld doesn't sell pretzels until after 4 p.m. The reason being that once you've had a pretzel, you're generally pretty full and don't feel like buying more overpriced food.

Fact #4: You can't get drinking straws at SeaWorld because the water birds eat them and die.

Fact #5 (and this is a good one): When the dolphins are in heat, the trainers close the observation pool as the dolphins sometimes derive sexual pleasure from throwing themselves against the walls of the pool and, on occasion, they have been known to accidentally fly out. And nothing will ruin your day at SeaWorld faster than being smacked in the face by a horny dolphin.

Like all theme parks, SeaWorld is essentially a small city with a very structured departmental government. With nearly twenty different departments from Food Service to Animal Care, the park administration saw fit to give each department its own standard-issue three-button colored work shirt so any employee could be immediately identified with his or her department. For example, the color for the Entertainment Department was black. Horticulture was navy blue, and Accounting wore a garish pink. To gaze upon the employee lunchroom was to behold a living Jackson Pollock painting: green shirts mingling with red shirts, a trio of black shirts in the corner, a mass of orange shirts lounging against the wall, an ever-morphing kaleidoscope.

The departments, represented by their colors, also had an unofficial coolness ranking amongst employees—a hierarchical pyramid of aspiration, if you will. At the bottom of the pyramid was the Operations department, or, as it was known, Ops. Light blue work shirt. Ops employees walked around the park with a broom and a waste can. They cleaned up barf. They were social pariahs.

Skipping up a couple rungs past the Merchandise and Ticketing departments, there was Food Service, the bourgeoisie of SeaWorld departments, where, for two summers during high school, I learned about the snack proclivities of Mr. and Mrs. Middle Class America as an assistant manager for the Shamu Land Area.

It was also during those two summers that I was briefly knocked unconscious by a low-flying duck. I had thought the duck was flying abnormally low, but a lot of ducks fly low at SeaWorld. I can tell you that it is well nigh impossible to look cool after one has just been leveled by a mallard, and if I ever see that duck again, I will fucking kill it.

After Food Service, you have the Horticulture department, populated by senior citizens and insanely hot college girls. The real sexpots of SeaWorld, however, were the water skiers. Toothsome and bronzed, they appeared to have been hired by seventh-grade boys. An invitation to one of the water skier's exclusive house parties was a badge you could wear the entire summer.

Near the very top of the social pyramid, without a doubt, were the animal trainers. Every freckle-faced fifteen-year-old working the Capt. Kidd Stuffed Animal Treasure Chest dreamed of one day shucking their light green work shirt for the cream colored v-neck tee of the Animal Care department. And really, the trainers were all very intelligent and nice people, but generally more comfortable communing with the dolphins or seals than other humans.

Ultimately, at the pinnacle of social prestige were the park emcees. In their two-toned collared shirts, the emcees were park celebrities. SeaWorld Ohio employed six or seven emcees that rotated through all of the shows from the Baywatch Water-Ski Adventure Show to the Hawaiian High Dive Luau. Most emcees gained a reputation for being better at one show than others. For instance,

Kelly was great in the High Dive show, but tongue-tied at the Hotel Clyde and Seamore, which required a fair amount of improvisation. Phil was pretty solid in the bird show, though never really got the requisite melodramatic flair required for the Shamu Show.

But Danny aced them all.

Tall and tan with an exceptional wit, Danny was a great performer. Everything worked when Danny was in the show. The corny bird jokes. The transitions. The false sense of patriotism when the bald eagle closed the show. Danny made it beautiful.

But I wasn't an emcee. I was a trainer and, as fate would have it, I was a *bird* trainer—a job that requires you to love birds, and furthermore to help other people love birds. The irony was not lost on me. And while I was proud of my cream colored v-neck tee, what the Vice President of Entertainment at SeaWorld doesn't tell you when you interview to be a trainer at the bird show is that ten percent of the job is doing the show and the other ninety percent of the job is cutting up rat meat and cleaning up bird shit.

Every morning, the first job of the day was to prepare the birds' food—and for birds of prey, that means rats. SeaWorld ordered their rats from a place called the Gourmet Rodent. The rats are shipped frozen and are guaranteed to be disease free. Each night, the last trainer to leave the shabby trailer where we kept both the birds and the supplies put fifty rats in a Rubbermaid tray to thaw in the fridge overnight. In the morning, two trainers prepared the rats—and by "prepared" I mean cut them up with a pair of scissors. To prepare a rat, you first cut off the rat's head. Then the feet. Then the tail. Cutting up the belly of the rat you then pull off the hide and remove the abdominal wall and gastrointestinal track. The birds, like pro athletes, only got the best cuts of meat. My hands smelled of death for that entire summer. No soap could entirely remove the smell of dead rat. One of the other trainers and I perfected a method of skinning the rats so as to keep the hide more or less intact. We took to making three or four of these little rat puppets every morning and then staging scenes from big musicals for the rest of the crew. We even made the rats little costumes. We did the marionette scene from *The Sound of Music* and "I Got No Strings" from *Pinocchio*.

It was all very sick and very wrong.

The Wild Wings Bird Show took place in a large circular stadium surrounded by soaring maple and fir trees. The stage was a bright green circle of AstroTurf with various poles and fake trees dotting the perimeter. The bird show was hosted by an emcee and two trainers—one for the birds of prey and one for the exotic birds—and a handful of other trainers hid throughout the stadium to catch and release birds at various points during the show. Essentially the emcee would start the show with a welcome and some lame bird jokes, introduce the two on-stage trainers, and then banter with them as they presented their respective flying critters. As hokey as the show was, the birds were amazing in action, swooping low over the crowd, their wings brushing against cheeks and noses, and then back high into the air. Audiences always lingered in the stands for a chance to see the hawks and owls and condors close up in the meet 'n' greet after the show.

My favorite part of the bird show was introducing the birds. Birds of prey are not the brightest of animals, and as such do not respond to their names. By the beginning of June, I began to experiment with re-naming the birds for each and every show, much to the chagrin of the emcee, who then had to use that name for the rest of the segment.

I started conservatively at first.

"Ladies and gentlemen, this is our bald eagle, Hillary Clinton!"

And then I got bolder.

"Now entering the stadium, our Harris's hawks, natives of the desert southwest, Spamhead and Chunkers!"

And bolder.

"Ladies and gentlemen, now entering the arena on silent and deadly wings, our Eurasian eagle owl, Roast Beef!"

This was generally a showstopper. People would laugh or look confused

Is that bird really named Roast Beef? and the emcee might pause or pointedly ask me for the bird's real name. But not Danny. Without missing a beat, Danny would look me in the eye and say, "Tell me about Spamhead and Chunkers, Matt. Is it true they hunt in packs?"

Danny was the best.

A couple weeks into June, Danny called a meeting and told all the trainers in a great rush of words that he had liver cancer and that it was terminal and that the doctors had given him three months to live. The pain was pretty severe sometimes and the narcotics he was on didn't really help. The only thing that really took away the pain was marijuana. A couple puffs, according to Danny, were more effective than two doses of Vicodin. Kyle, the hippie stage manager assigned to the bird show, took it upon himself to make sure that Danny always had a steady supply of good weed for the rest of the summer.

In the beginning of July, our red tailed hawk Timagen, distracted by a sparrow during a training session, abandoned his routine and flew into the park. In the ensuing Benny Hill chase sequence, I fractured my ankle jumping over a fence. Since I could no longer perform the show, Lori, the head trainer, assigned me to narrator duty at an exhibit called Bald Eagle Point. For the next month and a half, I sat on a stool and answered questions about bald eagles:

Mister, is it true that bald eagles have sex in the air?

No, that's actually a courtship behavior. Fertilization takes place on the ground and is known as a cloacal kiss.

Mister, did that eagle break your leg?

No, but eagles are very strong. One of the eagles sprained a trainer's arm last summer by just squeezing its talons a bit too hard.

Mister, what do eagles eat?

Children. Mostly children.

Despite the spazzy kids and gabby tourists, being with the eagles was really peaceful, especially in the mornings when the park was quiet and the birds would cluck softly to one another, stretching their broken wings in the sun. SeaWorld had six mature bald eagles that had all been seriously injured in the wild. Some had been shot by hunters. A couple had been hit by cars while scavenging road kill. One had been injured in a storm. They were beautiful animals, fierce and proud, and for a brief time we were together in our brokenness.

Around the time I broke my ankle, Danny took a leave of absence from SeaWorld. He intended to do some traveling with his partner, to see some more of the world before he died, but the cancer was moving too quickly and he wasn't strong enough to travel very far. Instead, he and his partner rented a bright red VW convertible for the rest of the summer. He called the trailer once in awhile and told us about the soap operas he was now addicted to. At the end of July, he rented a big carnival tent and threw himself a going away party—a living funeral—although he had to lie on a couch for much of it.

In mid-August, Lori told us that Danny was coming back for one last day of shows. He wanted to do his job one last time. We hadn't seen Danny in several weeks, and when he strode up to the trailer he was impossibly thin. He wore a wan smile, his complexion was jaundiced, and a cowboy hat covered his brittle and thinning hair. But the man was undaunted.

There were only two bird shows scheduled that particular Wednesday; attendance was usually down mid-week. The other trainers all agreed that that was a good thing, as Danny probably couldn't handle more than two twenty-five minute shows. At our morning meeting, Lori, who had known Danny the longest, informed the rest of the trainers that he would be performing both shows that day. No one objected.

The first show went well. Nothing unusual. The birds did what they were supposed to do, and the audience oooh-ed and ahhh-ed in all the right places.

When the gate to the stadium opened for the last show of Danny's life, the usual sea of tourists in tacky airbrushed shirts with their camera bags and strollers and screaming babies was missing. Instead, I watched from my post backstage as a cluster of navy blue shirts entered the stadium followed by a group of black shirts and then green and orange and yellow and maroon and white. Everyone had come to see Danny do the show. Everyone had come to see Danny do the show one last time.

After the show, after all the tears and hugs and laughs, I bumped into Danny and his partner on the way back to their convertible and we walked together for a moment.

Then Danny, the consummate performer, asked me, "Was it a good show?"

"It was a good show," I said.

"Good," he said, "I was afraid it was a little slow."

"No," I said. "It was a good show, Danny." And I wanted to tell him then how much I admired him. How his bravery, his love for life in the face of such terrible adversity would always be with me. How I hoped to conduct myself in times of trial with his same grace and aplomb.

But all I could say was, "I'll see ya around, Danny."

"Yeah," he said with a half smile. "See ya."

He died a couple weeks later.

At the end of the summer, the park closes to the public. All the food stands are winterized. Tarps are draped over the flower beds. The Muzak that courses through the thousands of hidden speakers is finally turned off. And at the bird show, all the birds are treated to several days of huge meals. A direct result of this feasting is a massive molt. The birds, instinctually sensing that they have enough calories to grow new feathers, drop their old ones, rendering themselves flightless for days. They do this because the future is uncertain and when fortune affords you a good meal and a warm perch you take advantage of it because Mother Nature, as any bird will tell you, makes no promises.

WHEN THE FAIRIES CAME

BY JULIE GANEY

I was ten years old when my mother revealed to me that there wasn't a Santa Claus.

We were lying on my parents' bed, and I remember running my finger along the wavy pattern stitched into the green velveteen bedspread over and over. Now, I'd asked my Mom for the truth about Santa, badgered her, actually, but when she finally admitted it, it was a blow. Rather than feeling vindicated that my suspicions were correct, I felt a little betrayed; a little lied to. I remember her saying that "the spirit of Christmas is real, and that's what's important," but I just wondered why the whole world was in on a conspiracy to get kids to believe in a big fat man in a red suit that didn't exist.

That's not what I was thinking about that June evening, though, as I sat with my neighbors, Jenny and Deb, on Jenny's front porch, drinking really cold pinot grigio. I was thinking about my garden, as we sat watching our kids playing in the front yard, eight of them between the three of us (but only one's mine, so it's all lopsided). Our husbands straggled out from time to time, joining us and leaving us as they pleased. The only remarkable things about the almost identical wood frame houses on our street in Rogers Park are the nice big front porches and the open front yards which connect all the way down the block, not broken up by fences or trees, where the kids chase each other and claim ownership of the entire block, as much as kids can these days when they have to be constantly watched.

On this particular night, the older kids, the tweens and teenagers, were next door on my own front porch, whispering and then laughing too loudly, posing a little for each other, even though they've known each other since they were babies. The littler kids, my own four-year-old and Jenny's five-year-old, Selena, were playing with sidewalk chalk in their own signature style, which involved garden hoses, buckets of water, and lots of chalk that was then mixed into a paste to be applied, thick and Van Gogh-like, to the sidewalk. The front yard was littered with the activities they'd already exhausted: bikes, a scooter, plastic dishes full of mud and leaves, a couple soccer balls.

Jenny glanced at over at her son on my porch. "I think Alex must have heard Michael and me having sex," she whispered. "Because he sleeps with his door shut every night now."

"There are all sorts of reasons an eleven-year-old boy sleeps with his door shut," Deb responded. "And they all have to do with sex."

We laugh and drink, and I notice my hands on the wine glass, wrecked from an afternoon in the garden, hacking away at plants that threaten to take over the entire yard. When we first moved into our house, I embraced gardening with more passion than skill, throwing everything I could lay my hands on into the ground. Now, five years later, the flowerbeds require constant pruning and dividing. I've even just dug stuff up and given it away on my front sidewalk with a cheery little sign that says, "Free perennials!" It's a part-time job from May to October keeping the vegetation at bay.

"Mom. We need something to do." It's my daughter, Dorothy. She approaches the porch, and kicks her filthy little foot against mine.

"Why don't you write a note to Bart and Karen on their sidewalk?" I suggest.

"We're tired of chalk," she whines.

Selena joins her at the foot of the porch steps, her little brown belly smeared with pink chalk. "We want something to eat. We're hungry," she angles.

"No," Jenny says. "No more snacks."

"Why don't you take your dollies for a walk?" I suggest.

"No," Dorothy says, irritated by our obtuseness. "They're *sleeping*." I look at her sweaty face and glassy eyes: it's obvious she's exhausted. The responsible thing to do would be to take her in, put her in a bath and then into bed—but I don't want to. I want to stay here chatting, admiring our children while they amuse themselves.

"Listen," I say. "Summer solstice is in a few days, when the fairies dance all night. Why don't you write them a note and invite them into our yards?"

Dorothy and Selena look to each other, eyes wide. "Yeah!" they say, and scramble up the stairs and into the house for paper and pens, which they bring out and fling in front of Jake and Katie, the two eight-year-olds. "We need you to help us write notes to the fairies," they announce, and splay themselves in the yard. Jenny gives me an impressed nod. This was perfect: an imaginative activity that invited an appreciation of nature and the invisible world, and was girly enough to sustain their interest.

An hour later, we pick up the yards and head inside for the night, but not before I tack two notes to the fairies on the big tree that stands between the sidewalk and the street in front of our house. Dorothy's note is full of pleas for friendship, and Selena's is full of questions: "Where do you live? How big are you? What do you eat?" They've collected some pretty rocks and clover as offerings to leave at the base of the tree.

Late that night, before I go to bed, I scrounge up some art paper. It looks woodlandy, with twigs and flower petals pressed into it, and, disguising my handwriting by using my left hand, I compose a note from the fairies:

> *Dear Children: We eat flower nectar and berries from your gardens while you're sleeping. We spend our time dancing, making flowers grow, and enjoying all things that are beautiful. We love living in your yards, because you are children who are very kind to each other.*

I tack the note to the big tree, taking the girls' letters, and go to bed. The next morning, there is squealing and wonder as the girls rush from the tree in their nightgowns and present the note to me to read for them. That evening, the same front porch ritual unfolds, and this time the fairies leave the girls a little garden of translucent lollipops in the front flowerbed, bedecked with ribbons and their names.

That's when fairy fever really kicked in.

Jake and Katie, the eight-year-olds, began writing notes at dusk as well. They were too old to truly believe in fairies, but they weren't stupid—it *always* makes more sense to participate in an enterprise that is supplying you with candy and ask the hard questions later. The kids demanded endless information from the fairies:

> *Dear Fairies: Do you know the tooth fairy? Do you know Mary and Fred, the bullfrogs that disappeared from the Foster's pond? Thank you for the candy, but could you please leave a magic wand? A real one? Can you turn little girls into fairies? Please take us to Fairyland with you. We are very good dancers.*

I started to get a little more inventive with my late night fairy notes:

> *Dear children: Yes we know the tooth fairy, but she is very busy and travels a lot. We like pretty rocks and flowers, but don't like squirrels. We're afraid it's too risky to leave you a magic wand,*

because the elves might come along and steal it. Yes, we know
Mary and Fred, they are dear frog friends, and lots of fun.

This last bit was tricky, because all the adults would bet money
that Noel, the Foster's own bloodthirsty cat, had massacred the frogs
but, like the fact that your parents have sex, this was information
those kids didn't really want.

I spent my late evenings devising methods for the fairies to
delight the girls: leaving tiny piles of fairy dust, or a trail of pebbles
leading to a basket of strawberries. At one point, Jenny, watching
her kids discover their names spelled out in sticks in the back yard,
offered vaguely, "Do you need any help with this?" But fairy work was
so gratifying! Look, no one can excel in every area of motherhood—
but this? This I could do!

Late one night, I found Dorothy, her forehead pressed against
the screen in her window, searching the yard below. "I can hear
them, but I can't see them," she said.

"Really?" I asked. "What do they sound like?"

"Oh, bells and whispering and stuff. Don't get near the
window." She waved at me. "They won't come out if grownups are
around. They just like kids."

One night around midnight, my husband Brad padded out
onto the front porch to find me teetering atop a stepstool in the wet
grass, tying pink ribbons to the branches of an overgrown hydrangea.

"What are you doing?" he asked sleepily.

"Well, I'm decorating this tree."

"No, really. What are you doing?" He sat down on the top step
of the porch. "This fairy stuff seems a little out of hand. I mean, they
really believe."

"Well, it's great that they believe," I said, "It's giving them an
experience of magic."

"Yeah, but it's untrue, Julie," he says carefully. "It's a lie."

"It's not a lie. Fairies don't exist, but magic does, and that's
what's important."

He rested his head on the banister, looked at me, his dark eyes weighted with sleep. "I'm just saying that you're creating a situation where it's completely irrational for them *not* to believe in fairies, because everything around them supports the idea, as much as everything supports the concept of gravity."

"Honey, don't overthink it." I took my ribbon scissors and began hacking away at the wild oregano under the tree. "Jesus, this stuff grows so fast you can see it. It's taking over the yard."

And then, as I heard Brad sigh and head inside, I thought of my mother and me on the green bedspread talking about Santa. How the depth and scope of that discovery had called everything into question in my ten-year-old mind: *What about the special Santa wrapping paper, the muddy footprint by the fireplace, the reindeer tracks we had seen on the sloping roof of the house?* And what if Brad was right? To discover the truth about fairies was to unravel something of magic in general, to untie a knot that won't hold anything together anymore. If fairies are a hoax, then there goes the Tooth Fairy. And if she's made up, why not the Easter Bunny, Santa, God, for that matter? Santa and God have a lot in common, with their white beards and the keeping track of whether you're good or not, but God, poor *God*. When was the last time He showed up at the mall? I sat there on the stepstool, the oregano bleeding perfume at my feet, realizing that there's no way to unplant a seed a once it's rooted and taken hold, unless you want to leave a gaping hole.

The next day, after the ribbon tree had been celebrated and danced around, it became clear that another corner had been turned. I arrived home in the middle of the day to find Dorothy and Selena in their swimsuits on the front sidewalk, screaming at the sky.

"Fairies, we see you! Come down here!"

As I got out of the car, Dorothy yelled, "Mom, look! The fairies are writing in the sky!" I looked up to see a skywriting plane high in the air leaving an unintelligible trail of white smoke against the clear blue sky. Selena and Dorothy continued their hoarse screaming, their little bodies rigid with passion, the sprinkler running and forgotten in the yard. I joined Brad, who was sitting on the porch swing watching them.

"Did you tell them the plane exhaust was fairy writing?' I asked.

He shook his head, incredulously.

"What's it say, Mom? What does it say?" Dorothy demanded.

"I don't know," I shrugged, helplessly.

Over the next few days, Dorothy and Selena became obsessed with visiting Fairyland. Somehow they got the idea that they could go at night, in their sleep, and that if they drank enough of what they called "special potion," limes squeezed into water, they would start shrinking. Dorothy demanded to be measured several times a day, proclaiming, "I feel like I'm getting shorter, Mom, I really do!" Then, Selena announced that she had actually gone to Fairyland during the night. After that they would no longer eat cantaloupe because, in Fairyland, it tasted like poop.

The summer wore on, the blackberry bushes took over the lavender in the garden, and the notes to the fairies continued, their tone changing a bit, becoming less plaintive and a little more demanding: "Why can't we see you? Why are you hiding? Will you leave us money?" I started not answering their notes sometimes, but that didn't slow the girls down. As Dorothy's fifth birthday approached at the end of August, she became obsessed with the fairies attending her party. Hyped up on magic, she wanted a magician to come and do a show in our backyard.

The day of her birthday was beautiful, the cake covered in flowers, the magician a good sport, taking the time to show some of his tricks to Dorothy afterwards. That night, entering her room to tuck her in, I found her, once again, forehead against the screen, searching the yard below.

"Hey," I said, sitting on the edge of the bed.

She pulled away from the window and looked at me.

"Did you have a nice party, honey?"

"Mmm-hmm." She reached out her finger and ran it across the screen.

"Did you like the magician?"

"Well, I wanted a *real* magician. One who could do the real magic, not just tricks. And the fairies didn't come. They never come. They never let us see them."

Her brow furrowed over her heavy, tired eyes, as her face filled with desperation, a longing that took me forward in time to when she would be a teenager and would want a boy she couldn't have, or when she'd be older than that, wanting all manner of things that people and fairies could not deliver.

"Do you think they're really out there, Mom?" she asked.

"What do you think?" I countered.

"I don't know."

A few days later, the fairies would leave a final note, wishing the kids on the block a good school year, bidding them goodbye, as they fled the cool weather in a clumsy, unsatisfying exit.

But that night, the night of Dorothy's birthday, we lay down together, my face buried in her hair that smelled vaguely of cake, listening to what we could almost hear through the window: the plants groaning over their borders in the garden, and the fairies packing their bags. 🪑

PUSH KICK COAST
BY RIC WALKER

Push, kick, push, kick, push, kick, coast.

I was never a good skater, but I'd push kick coast for the ladies in the USA—the United Skates of America. During the last days of roller disco, 1980, I was a man of fifteen living it up in Shaker Heights, Ohio, a Cleveland suburb. Well, not yet a man, but Stacy Wynn and Herman Armour could legally drive and Jeff Jones and I were only a summer away from learner's permits.

And, oh, what a summer it promised to be: no day camp, no summer school, no Vacation Bible School. My little sister was staying with our grandparents for the summer. Both my brothers were in the military and my single mother's schedule as a nurse made my curfew impossible to enforce. The world was my oyster, and the United Skates of America was my oyster bed.

The old USA on the East Side of Cleveland was the place where teenage romance was born. From the outside, it looked like a brick airplane hangar. Once inside the double set of heavy barn doors, the bulk of the space was a wooden roller rink set into the far left corner. To the right of the rink were bathrooms and flashing pinball machines. To the immediate left of the entrance was the skate rental, and then the refreshment area, complete with year-old hot dogs rolling under a heat lamp. The proximity of food and skate rental made it easy for the same employee to go straight from handing out skates to slapping a dog on a bun. When I was fifteen, this never struck me as disgusting.

Between the rink and refreshments was a carpeted area with chewing gum smashed in the floor that looked like smooth black pebbles scattered around. Benches made out of those giant wooden spools for telephone cable, cut in half and nailed to the floor, covered with shag carpeting. They were random colors: red, orange, yellow. The area looked like a psychedelic mushroom garden.

With one skate atop a mushroom cap, I forced a casual pose that only looks cool to department store catalog photographers. Wearing my favorite polyester disco shirt designed with a photorealistic pattern of a sunset view from the dock o' the bay (the top three buttons strategically left open) and my tightest Jordache jeans, I was feeling good. I was convinced of my own manliness because I was already six feet tall, but my baby face and irrepressible smile told the world I was still a kid. Looking cool, I shared my pack of Rolos with one of the two cute girls from Cleveland Heights that Stacy Wynn and I had just met.

My man, Stacy Wynn. He was a year older than me and ten years cooler, definitely the coolest dude in our four-man crew. At five foot eleven, Stacy was an inch shorter than me, but if you took our Afros into consideration, he stood nearly an inch taller. He was the only guy I have ever met named Stacy. He didn't care that he had a girl's name. "It helps me relate to women better," he would say. Stacy was cool like that.

He was the first kid I ever met who seemed truly comfortable with himself. Out of the four of us, he was the biggest ladies' man, too, and he would help you upgrade your skills. He had unusually savvy advice for a sixteen-year-old. I remember him warning me about trying to be funny all the time. "Ric, you're so light-skinned and pretty, girls love you, until you open up your mouth. Girls like to see you have a serious side, even if you don't," he said. He had acne-free brown skin and a wide easy smile that made you believe everything he said, no matter how outlandish.

Stacy lightly touched the forearm of one of the Cleveland Heights cuties, "Have you seen my man Ric here on *Days of Our Lives*? Yeah, he's an actor."

Cutie #2: "Uhh, no. . ."

Rolo-eating cutie: "Oh, I thought you looked familiar."

Stacy: "Yeah, he's off for the summer 'cuz we're working on a movie deal. I'm his agent."

Stacy said stuff like that with so much confidence that even I almost believed it. It wasn't so much that Stacy was lying, it was more his sense of humor. He wanted to see how far he could take a joke. You could always count on him to tell the truth when it really mattered, like when you needed to wipe your nose or a blast of Binaca or if your underwear was peeking over the top your jeans. (I grew up in a time when exposed underwear was considered embarrassing to a teen.)

As I offered another Rolo, I spotted Jeff Jones push kicking toward us. His eyes locked with mine from across the refreshment area and, as usual, he looked serious. Little Jeffy Jones was my oldest friend. I don't remember a time *before* knowing Jeff. He was so short he disappeared behind people as he skated, but what Jeff lacked in height he made up for in width. He was like a mini-Schwarzenegger, built like a fireplug; we used to say that when he was a baby, his mom gave him twenty-pound rattles.

On the street we grew up on, we used to say that Jeff had "Gremlin blood." If he got angry, he got super strong. It was easy to get him to laugh, but he never made jokes himself—always serious.

Jeff rolled up beside me. "Somebody's messing with Herm," he said, referring to the fourth guy in our set.

As I push kicked away from the Heights Cuties, I heard Stacy behind me saying, "We're coming back for those numbers, ladies." He was smooth like that.

The fact that somebody was messing with Herman was no surprise—that happened on the regular. Herman Armour, whom I had known since he was eight, was five foot six and about twelve pounds, and most of that weight from his very big mouth. He was also the first kid I ever saw talk back to adults. He had an acidic wit and was quick to humiliate others—a technique we dubbed "The Herman Burn."

Push, kick, coast.

When we got to the far end of the mushroom benches, a small crowd had already formed, hoping for a fight. There were two guys menacing Herman: Tre and Vance. Tre, the leader, was one of those guys who looked mad even when he laughed. Seventeen, athletic, and nearly six feet tall, even taller in his candy apple red skates. His sidekick, Vance, was thin and even taller with an enormous 'fro. We knew these guys from the USA, and they were punks.

Jeff worked his way past a couple of people so he could stand right beside Tre and Vance in case anything went down. Classic Jeff, he always had your back. The verbal exchange was half threats, half Herman Burns.

Tre: "You talk to my girl again, I'ma bust you up."

Herman: "I don't talk to Vickie. We just like to exercise lips."

"You better shut up, you little faggot."

"If I'm a faggot, your girlfriend's a dude."

Both Herman and Tre were playing for the crowd—just using contrasting styles. As usual, Herman was getting laughs. Tre looked around at the cackling crowd. His thick lips narrowed and his brow dropped. He was about to kill Herman. I tried to use a Jedi mind trick to make Herman shut up. It didn't work. Herman repeated to the crowd, "His girlfriend's a dude!" Everybody laughed.

Except Tre, who took a step toward Herman. The growing crowd fell silent. "I am going to kick your little ass."

"You're going to kiss my little what?"

"Ass! I'ma kiss yo' little a—" Tre didn't get to finish his sentence. The howling crowd helped him realize his mistake. There were people clapping or slapping fives or literally falling down with laughter. There is nothing funnier to a teenager than another's humiliation.

At this point, Tre's options to save face were limited. Personally, I would have broken off a spate of "Yo Momma" jokes. First, I would ridicule her weight, then focus on her stupidity, and finish off with a diatribe on her sluttiness, but this technique of deflection was not a part of Tre's repertoire. Nope, he wasn't a joker; he was a man of action.

Using the full force of his sinewy arms, Tre pushed Herman back. Herman, caught off guard because he was basking in the laughter of the crowd, went down hard, skidding on the carpet enough for a real Herman Burn. The force of the push caused Tre to glide backwards on his skates, arms extended to either side of body like a human cross that asks, "Whatcha gonna do?"

Some kids rolled away from the action but with a push-kick, Stacy coasted into the middle of it, always the peacemaker. Stacy liked things light. He liked to have fun. This wasn't fun. Stacy said, "Re-lax."

That is when Sidekick Vance tried to roll in, too, but Jeff stuck out his foot. Sidekick Vance's skate didn't go where he expected. He spun on his other skate and in an effort to maintain his balance, Vance grabbed the closest thing, which just happened to be Janice Hall's enormous left breast. Janice, the toughest girl I ever met, was not in skates. "Uh-uh!" she yelled and then started swinging, beating Sidekick Vance to the ground. Hilarious. This brought cheers from the crowd and security guards into the situation.

Within seconds, Tre and Vance were being escorted from USA. "I am gonna get you!" Tre yelled with an employee on his arm.

Herman couldn't resist delivering one more dig before Tre was out the door: "Well, I'll be at Amy Joy's eating donuts with yo momma!"

"Ooooo!" went the crowd, and then quickly broke off into small groups to recount the drama. "Shut up more often," Stacy said, smacking Herman on the back of his neck. "Damn." And with a push kick, Stacy coasted through the crowd toward a group of girls, slapping Jeff five as he passed. With a relieved smile on my face, I turned to the right and ordered a hot dog.

The USA closed at 11 p.m. As always, after skating, we drove to Amy Joy Donuts in Herman's big-ass Buick Electra 225, a car I named the Boat Mobile. All the way there, Herman and I were trading insults the way two kids play catch. Because Herm couldn't parallel park, we went to the deserted lot out back and parked in one of the few pools of light.

We took the short walk to donut heaven. The still night air was that perfect temperature that is impossible to feel, neither hot nor cold, but weather equivalent to being weightless. It was silent except for Stacy and Herman's footsteps twenty feet ahead and the sound of Jeff and I taking turns punching each other in the arm medium-hard for no apparent reason. I heard someone ahead of us say, "Hey, hey, you got somethin' to say now, pussy?"

It was Tre with a four-man posse. They had been waiting, maybe for hours, to ambush us. I recognized Tre and Sidekick Vance, but the other three were complete strangers to me. There was Ugly Thug, Fat Thug, and this *old* dude with squinty eyes who must have been twenty-five.

"W'chew gonna say now, huh?" demanded Tre. Of course, Herman didn't have anything to say—no crowd, no glory, no point— but Stacy didn't miss a beat. He stepped forward with both palms extended and said, "Aww, c'mom now fellas."

But that was the end of the conversation and time stopped. Time stopped everything but action. They rushed at us—Sidekick Vance tackled Herman, but the first guy to get to Stacy caught a mouthful of knuckles for his trouble. Tre and Fat Thug piled onto Stacy, then Jeff dove into that pile-up headfirst.

Me? I stood frozen in time, stunned, but what brought me

back to the moment was the flash of pain in my jaw that told me I had just been clocked. I didn't know see who had struck me, but standing over me was Ugly Thug winding up to kick me. But then, flying into my field of vision, a blur that roared named Jeffrey Jones. He rang that stranger's bell. Gremlin blood!

Ugly Thug tried to cover his ears and face as Jeff, using his knee to pin Ugly Thug down, rained down haymakers just often enough to make him a little uglier and keep him addled. I rushed to help Herm, who was on his belly getting his face pushed into the blacktop with Sidekick Vance on his back. I threw my arm around Vance's neck and pulled, but the angle made the headlock a chokehold, so when I pulled harder, Vance made a panicked, gravelly sound as he strained for air. As Vance struggled against my grip, Herm was up instantly, throwing rabbit punches at Vance's ribs saying, "What now, bitch?" I released Vance, who fell into a ball.

And then: *CLOP!* That's what it sounded like, over my right shoulder, *clop*, like a percussionist's wood blocks. A sound so sudden, strange, and out of place, everyone froze for a moment. Then, in sync, everyone turned to the source of the sound and saw Stacy collapse, making absolutely no attempt to break his own fall, his head clapping the blacktop like the last domino. The old dude with the squinty eyes stood over Stacy. His nostrils flared, smile twisted. In his hands was a wooden ball bat.

Tre's guys scattered. We ran to our friend. Stacy lay motionless. I expected to see blood, but there wasn't any—just the seed of the knot that would later grow on the side of his head. If he'd had a blanket you'd think he was having a sad dream.

"Stacy! Stacy!"

"Don't shake him like that, Herm," Jeff commanded.

"Wake up, Stacy, man."

"What are we going to do?" I asked.

"He'll be all right," asserted Herman. And why wouldn't he be? In our suburban world everything turned out okay, right?

After what seemed like a lifetime, Stacy opened his eyes but didn't focus or answer questions. I asked, "What year is it?"

"What are you talking about?" Herman chided.

"I don't know!"

Then Jeff stated, "We're taking him to the hospital."

"No, he'll be alright. Besides," Herman argued. "We'll get in trouble, the police, your dad, my parents will kill me."

This debate went on entirely too long. I broke the tie by saying, "The hospital."

On the way to the ER, Stacy was laid across the back seat of the Electra 225, head on my lap, legs on Jeff's. I looked down into his face. His normally keen eyes rolled unfocused. He was not crying, but tears flowed back into his hair. I felt so hot I wanted to stick my head out of one of the open windows to catch my breath. I forced a joke over the sound of the wind in the car: "I have never seen your 'fro so jacked up, the nurses are going to be disappointed." In a lucid moment, Stacy looked me in the eyes and said, "I got mine, didn't I? I got mine." At the time, I thought Stacy meant he got in a few good punches, but now I think it was not about violence but of finding peace. "I got mine."

Then Stacy had a single convulsion. Even his convulsion was cool. Just a push on my hand, a kick of his legs, then he coasted, coasted away for the very last time. Push, kick, coast. ▉

CRAZY FOR YOU
BY LOTT HILL

When I was eighteen, I fell in love with a Catholic schoolgirl. *Mmmm hmmm.* Her name was Amy Richardson, and she was the most beautiful thing I'd ever seen. She was perfect from her Mary Lou Retton smile to the two freckles above her left knee, in the space between her high socks and the hem of that little plaid skirt. Ohhh that little plaid skirt! And she could sing too. Had a voice like an angel! Or so *I* thought. Amy was the lead in her high school musical, which also starred my best friend, Laura. On opening night, I sat front row center in that high school gymnasium with its makeshift stage and folding chairs, and the rest of the world just fell away. It felt as if she sang every song just for me and that the universe had conspired to bring us to that one perfect moment of her performance. In my eyes, she was already a superstar, and I was her biggest fan.

Maybe I should stop here and fill you in on a couple of important details. The first thing you should know is that I'm kind of gay. Okay, maybe not *kinda* gay, but *really* gay. I had just come out a few months before I met Amy and had dated only one guy who broke my heart. And though you may think that I was confused, or trying to deny my sexuality, or even that I was on the rebound, this wasn't some my-heart-was-shattered-by-a-guy-and-now-I'm-going-to-go-back-to-girls sort of thing: I was really head-over-heels in love with Amy from the moment I saw her, and it just felt like the real thing. (And her voice—both simultaneously vulnerable and confident—reminded me a little bit of Madonna.)

Anyhow, the second thing you should know is that I was in my second semester of college and Amy was a junior in high school. I know, I know, it sounds like I was robbing the cradle, but this *was* *Kentucky*! And that's what we do there. For real.

The third thing is that the production my friend and Amy were in was *Godspell*. You know, *Godspell*, the musical based on the Gospel of Matthew? Think *Hair*, but with Jesus, John the Baptist, and Judas. You get the picture. It *was* a Catholic girls' school after all and, as I mentioned before, Amy was playing the lead role. That's right: *she was Jesus*!

Her costume was a blue Superman t-shirt, rainbow suspenders, and blue jeans, and even though she was kinda small, it seemed like she filled up the whole stage as she sang, "When wilt thou save the people, oh God of mercy, when?" I could never really carry a tune, but I loved to sing, and while helping my friend Laura rehearse, I had learned all the songs by heart. And I wasn't religious or anything—God knows the Catholic church wouldn't have *me*—but watching Amy on stage, I felt like I was being filled with the Holy Spirit, and that night, I swear, I would have dropped to my knees and accepted Jesus as my savior.

To me, each song sounded better than the one before, and it didn't matter that there was no stage lighting or that the set was mostly made up of cardboard boxes; I was captivated all the way up to the very end when Jesus/Amy was tied to the cross with red silk sashes. The other players circled around and genuflected, her head—adorned with a wreath of grape vines—drooped to one side as her sparkling mahogany hair cascaded in front of her face. Her chin trembled, and she sang ever so softly, forlornly, "Oh, God. I'm dying." And the others writhed on their knees answering in song, "Oh, God, you're dying." And when Amy looked up at the audience to sing her final line, her eyes met mine, her lips quivered, as she sang in a whisper: "Oh, God. I'm dead."

And one single perfect tear escaped from her right eye. She didn't look away, and with her nailed to the cross and me in a metal folding chair right at the front of the gymnasium, I felt a tear roll down my cheek and my heart swelled for poor Jesus and this amazing girl, for all of humanity. And just before she shut her eyes and dropped her chin to her chest, I detected the faintest hint of a smile on her lips. A smile for me. Oh God, indeed!

I attended the show the next night. And the next. It only played three times that weekend, but I was there in the same seat all three shows. On the second night, Amy noticed me halfway through her first song, and on the third, I could tell that she came onto the stage looking for me. Afterward, I waited as Amy made her rounds to family and friends, and then shyly toed her way over to me. "Hey," she said.

"Hey," I said.

"How'd you like the show?" she asked.

"I was here all three nights."

"I noticed."

Now, you gotta realize that I'm not a player, and I certainly wasn't very slick at that age. Oh, I tried, with my jeans pegged tightly at my ankles and my popped collar, but I wasn't fooling anyone. But somehow I was running on automatic pilot when Amy was around, and I managed to ask: "I'm going to get something to eat with Laura. You wanna come with?"

Amy's face dropped. "I can't." And then she said it: "I'm supposed to meet my boyfriend."

I know! That felt like a blow to my gut. A boyfriend? I hadn't seen a boyfriend any of the three nights I'd been stalking this girl. A *boyfriend*? The possibility hadn't even crossed my mind, but of course a girl this perfect would have a boyfriend!

Those next few days were miserable for me. Throughout the weekend I had been bouncing off the walls singing songs from *Godspell*, but now I was in a gloomy funk. But then, out of the blue, Amy got my number from Laura and called to see if I would like to get together. I was floored and quickly agreed to meet her on Saturday afternoon at the mall. As soon as we met up, Amy insisted that we go to Soundtracks, complaining that she could never get her boyfriend to take her there. Anybody remember Soundtracks at the mall? They were like little recording studios for karaoke where you'd pick out a song, sing along, and then you could buy the tape. I told her that I couldn't sing very well, but she didn't care. She was just thrilled I was willing to go with her. We flipped through the songbooks looking for duets, but because we were on our first date, we picked kind of a safe one: Madonna's "Crazy For You."

(I know, I know.)

Inside, the recording booth was small and close, and we gazed into each other's eyes over the microphone we shared. Through the bulky headphones we both wore, her voice reverberated in my head. The heat coming from our two bodies made we wonder if the recording booth might burst into flames. Again I felt like I did on that first night I'd seen her: like we were the only two people in the world. Later, I got up the nerve to ask about her boyfriend, and she confessed they'd been drifting apart. Then she asked if I was seeing anyone. I told her no, but the last person I dated was a guy. She said she knew, and that it didn't matter, and I wondered if my heart would explode before I ever got the chance to kiss this girl. But in that recording booth, I didn't worry about any of that, not her boyfriend, not my ex-boyfriend, not the fact that I couldn't sing very well.

And for the record, we didn't kiss that day. It was our first date, and she technically still had a boyfriend, but that wouldn't last for long. See, someone had seen Amy and me at the mall and had started a story that made it back to her boyfriend in about fifty-two hours, and he'd gone and told Amy's parents that he was worried that she was being led astray by some older guy . . . who was gay.

And as you might guess, that went over really well in a severely Catholic household. That was all Amy's parents needed to forbid her from ever seeing me again.

The fact that she promptly broke up with her boyfriend was little consolation in light of this decree from her parents. But you can't cage love. She called me after her parents went to bed, and we tried to think of someplace we could meet where no one would know us, like a park on the other side of town, or the bus station, or the cemetery but, finally, we came up with the perfect place: the Burlington Coat Factory.

Oh yes, the Burlington Coat Factory in a strip mall on the other side of town. We could drive there separately and browse among the coats while we made sure no one we knew was in the store. Then we'd meet along the back wall where we'd walk among long raincoats, sport coats, overcoats, trench coats, cashmere, camel hair, fur. Usually she'd be wearing that little plaid skirt and we'd stroll up and down the aisles, holding hands and talking. Sometimes we'd pretend to be browsing, but after refusing half-hearted *May I help you*s from the bored salespeople, we'd just loiter in some corner and make out.

We met like that three or four times, always at the Burlington Coat Factory, pressing our bodies together among the coats, until one day when Amy said that it wasn't enough. She didn't care what her parents thought about it, she loved me and she wanted to see me someplace normal, someplace where we weren't surrounded by so many ugly coats. The next weekend was Easter, and she had a plan.

On Easter Sunday, Amy pretended to be sick so she didn't have to go with her family to her grandmother's house and, once her parents left, she headed over to my house. That afternoon was the first time that Amy and I had been outside together, as a couple. The spring sun, holding hands, watching my nephew hunt for the Easter eggs we had hidden, it was perfect.

Eventually, my family took my nephew to the zoo, and Amy and

I stayed behind at my house. Finally we were alone. In my bedroom. Kissing. Pressing together, making our way toward the bed. It felt like steam was rising from our bodies and suddenly Amy was over me, on top of me, and guiding my hand inside her soft sweater. In a heavy whisper she told me she wanted to make love.

"Have you ever?" I asked.

"No," she said. "But if I get pregnant, there's no way my family can keep us apart. They'll have no choice but to let us get married."

Married.

My whole future flashed before my eyes: Amy pregnant; twelve kids by the time I'm twenty-one; working at the Burlington Coat Factory watching kids sneaking around and making out; no more college for me; no college for Amy and, of course, she could never have a brilliant musical career if she started having babies at sixteen. Her words rang in my ears: *They'll have no choice but to let us get married.* What is it with the Catholics?

Besides, truth be told, there was something missing. (Get your mind out of the gutter—I'm not talking about *that*! Well, maybe your dirty mind is somewhat right, but that wasn't all.) Even though I *could* imagine a future with Amy, I couldn't imagine it *that way*, starting there with children and a shotgun wedding and a vow to stay with this one person for the rest of my life.

I pulled my hand out from under her sweater. "I don't want you to have to choose between them and me."

Amy pleaded, "But *I* choose you. I *want* you."

I guess this was the true test of my sexuality, or maybe, of my *morality*, because here I had this gorgeous Catholic schoolgirl on top of me, offering me her virginity, and I didn't take her up on it; even though this *was Kentucky*, I was just eighteen and couldn't imagine spending my entire life with only one person. And what's more, I knew I couldn't promise to be faithful to a woman. And how could I allow her to give her entire life to me if I couldn't do the same?

"But I love you," she argued.

"And I love you too. That's how I know we can't do this."

Amy was crying when she left my house. Easter Sunday, and I had made Jesus cry.

Three weeks later, the very last time I saw Amy, she had called and said, "I need to see you." We decided to meet in an hour . . . at the Burlington Coat Factory. In the back corner. Men's Big & Tall. Raincoats. She had on dark sunglasses. When she lifted them, I could tell that she had been crying. "I love you," she said. "*I'm crazy for you*. I don't know how to live without you."

"I know," I said. "But you've got your whole life ahead of you, and I don't ever want to be responsible for coming between you and your family."

"I know," she nodded. "I wanted to give you this." She handed me a cassette tape. I could see from the cover that she had recorded it in the mall at Soundtracks. She rose on her tiptoes and gave me one last sweet long kiss, and I knew it was over. There is no mistaking a real goodbye kiss.

I lingered among the big and tall raincoats to give her enough time to leave the store and the parking lot. I didn't want that kiss to be followed by anything, not even a last wave goodbye. I was afraid I'd do anything to make up for her tears. In my car, I popped the cassette into the tape player, but kept the windows rolled up as the first notes of "Crazy for You" began to play. It was Amy's voice. And she was singing just for me.

THIS TEACHER TALKS TOO FAST

BY MEGAN STIELSTRA

When I first started teaching, I thought it would go like *Dead Poets Society*: we'd rip up our textbooks, quote Whitman, play soccer to opera music, and if ever anyone was in trouble I'd know just how to save them.

That was a decade ago, and I've gotten more realistic. College textbooks are expensive, so there's no way we'd rip them up; and my students don't listen to opera, they listen to emo; and I can't save anybody. I teach creative writing—voice, structure, point of view; none of that's going to help Rachel, who's pregnant, or Kyle with the antidepressants, or Dennis who's *way* more interested in pot than he is in class, and I have these days sometimes where it's like, *What the hell am I doing?* This past semester was especially rough, and on the last day, as I was packing my things for winter break, I thought, *I could walk away.*

What if I walked away?

On the way out, I grabbed my mail—memos, a stack of student work, and a book. I checked the cover—some lit journal from a community college—and was all set to toss it when I noticed a page was marked with a post-it note. I opened it to a short story, saw the name of author, and stopped. In order to explain what happened next, I need you to imagine that I'm a character on *Grey's Anatomy*. I'm thinking specifically of the episode where Izzie gives up being a doctor—she's got eight million dollars from her dead fiancé, and she goes to say goodbye to Dr. Burke, who first taught her how to do a running whip stitch, and she tells him, "I'm sorry," 'cause it's her fault he got shot and has a tremor in his hand and maybe can't be surgeon anymore, and he says, "Don't you be sorry because of me. You have two good hands, and you're not using them, be sorry for that!" At this point, some pop song by a new up-and-coming artist starts playing and Izzie's face jerks as though she's been slapped. She stands there, confused and frozen in Burke's office until slowly, slowly, she looks down at her hands, holding them in front of her like she's about to play the piano. She studies every finger, every wrinkle, and turns them so the palms face upwards. We stare at those hands, all of us, imaging the thousands of lives they might save, and the camera pans back to Izzie's face, her lovely blue eyes wide and determined. *My God, what am I doing?* she thinks. *How can I give up becoming a surgeon?* and then, the song crescendos or maybe the chord changes in some significant way and—she smiles. It all becomes clear. She's not going to quit! She's going to stay, and be a great doctor! And here, here is the important part: it might never have happened if it hadn't been for Burke getting shot.

Just like that lit journal in my mailbox means nothing unless I tell you about Andrew.

It was my second year of teaching. I was twenty-three and still naive enough to think we could all recite Whitman standing on our desks— except we don't have desks in the Fiction Writing Department at Columbia College Chicago, we sit in semicircles so you can look everyone in the eye. It was the first day of class, and I was calling out attendance.

"Elizabeth?"

"Here."

"Angela?"

"Here."

"Andrew—?"

"Andrew—?"

I looked up. "Andrew—?" and I will never forget this; he said, "I'm fuckin' here already." This guy was nineteen, South Side Irish Catholic, complete with the accent, very baggy jeans belted just below his crotch, and these giant headphones that he would not turn off unless you told him to, like, "Andrew, we're starting class, can you lose the Eminem please?"

"Whatever," he'd say, which was all he ever said.

"Whatever," when we talked about Baldwin.

"Whatever," when we discussed student work.

"Whatever," when I told him he was failing. It was the fifth week of classes, and he'd missed three already. When he did show, it was an hour late, headphones blaring, sitting in the back of the room a good ten feet away from the rest of us in our semicircle, and it's very, very difficult to continue reading Faulkner under those circumstances. Had I been the teacher I am now, I'd have told Andrew he could join us after the break, but then? I wanted to save everybody.

"So if you don't care about failing," I asked, "Why are you still coming to class?"

Andrew's hair hung past his nose—I wanted to tell him to move it so I could look him in the eye. "My mom'll freak out if I don't," he said.

"This is college," I said. "Your mother doesn't—"

"Look, I fucking paid for the class," he said. "I'm fucking gonna come to it." In that moment, I was afraid of Andrew—not that I thought he'd hurt me physically, but that maybe he could tell I didn't have a clue what I was doing.

"Fine," I said. "But you have to write. We're a third of the way through the semester and you haven't given me any writing and—"

While I was talking, he stood up and opened his backpack, taking out a couple typed pages and dropping them in my lap.

Then he was gone.

His writing was really, really good, and it was about a guy who wanted to kill himself.

Now, lots of students write about suicide, but for some reason this felt different. It didn't feel like fiction. Usually, in such situations, you've got three options:

1. Ignore it, which really isn't an option so far as I'm concerned, so—

2. Contact somebody who knows what they're doing. I called the college's counseling hotline—and, for the record, I felt like a total asshole, like I was ratting out this guy's creative work, but me being an asshole was better than him being dead. Turns out, there's all sorts of legal implications to this stuff. This is college. Andrew is an adult—he has to choose to seek out counseling. I could suggest it but not enforce it, which brings me to—

3. Talk to Andrew directly.

Halfway through each semester, we do one-on-one conferences with every student—an hour-long sit-down to go over the strongest elements in their work. These are held in closet-sized cubicles in a hallway off the Fiction Writing Office, which is good because of the privacy, but also a little unnerving. Picture you and a semi-stranger locked up in a bathroom for an hour. Now picture Andrew and me during his conference, the two of us in this tiny, cramped space, and I'm making suggestions for his writing, like, "Could you maybe slow down the scene? Right here, when the character is taking all those pills and drinking all the vodka?" Because that's my job, right? To focus on his work? And then say something very subtle that'll inspire him to seek help on his own? Well, it is *not, not, not* that simple because sometimes those perfect words get all stuck in your throat, and you end up saying the absolute worst thing possible, like: "So. How're you *doing?*"

"Fine," he said.

"Fine?" I said. "Like, really fine?"

I couldn't see his eyes through the hair, but I knew he was looking at me like I was nuts. "Okay," I said. "Look. Do you need to . . . talk to somebody? I mean, there are people here who—" just like last time, he was on his feet and packing up. "Andrew!" I said. I wanted to reach out and grab his arm but figured that touching him would be as far from appropriate as I could get. "I'm just trying to help!"

He turned and faced me then. "It's fucking *fiction*," he said. "Isn't that what this is? A fucking *fiction* class?" And then he was gone.

I sat there in the cubicle for a really long time. I don't remember my exact train of thought, but it went something like: *Why can't I get through to him? How do I reach him? How do I save him?* I didn't know then what I do now: his life was so much bigger than my little one class a week. Think back for a second to when you were a freshman in college. What were you the most focused on?

Me? My folks were splitting up, my boyfriend back in Michigan was seeing somebody else, and I shared a twelve-by-twelve foot dorm room with a girl looped on Ecstasy four nights out of the week, I tell you what, teachers were the *last* thing on my mind.

My job is to help their writing, not to save their lives.

Right?

I gave Andrew an F, and on the last day of class I asked him to stay after. "You failed to fulfill the standards and policies of this class," I told him. "It doesn't mean that you're not a good writer."

"Whatever," he said. "I'm done with this school bullshit anyhow—" and then, like always, he was gone.

At the end of every semester, teachers turn in grades and all copies of student work to the Fiction Writing Department's office, at which time we're given our student evaluations. I flipped through the stack and found one that hadn't been filled out except for a single line in Andrew's handwriting. It said: *I can't smoke pot before this class. This teacher talks too fast.*

I thumbtacked that evaluation to my wall and looked at it for a while. Then, I put it in a box under my bed. *Shake it off,* I told myself. *New students, new chapter.* The first day of the spring semester I walked into class, called out attendance.

"Kelly?"

"Here."

"LaTasha?"

"Here."

"Brian—?"

"Brian—?"

"*Brian*—?" I looked up and it was *total déjà vu.* Same baggy pants, same headphones, same accent even! Except this wasn't Andrew. It wasn't Andrew. It was Brian, slouching in his seat and looking at me like *All right, sweetheart. What are you gonna do for me?*

He didn't show up the second week of class.

He didn't show up the third week.

On the fourth week he rolled in an hour late and sat down in the back of the room. That's when I sort of lost my mind. "All right, out in the hall," I told him. "Everybody else—read something, or . . . something." As I left the classroom, I tried to calm down. *This is not Andrew,* I told myself. *Don't put Andrew on this guy.*

"I'm sorry," he said, moving the hair out of his face. He had blue eyes. "The past couple weeks have been a nightmare."

"I'm sorry," I said. "But that doesn't excuse—"

"My friend killed himself," he said. "It's not your problem, I know, I just told you so you don't think I'm slacking off."

I said I'd help him catch up after class.

"Thank you," he said. "But actually, my friend? He was a student here. And I know they've got some of his work in the office and I was wondering if you could get it for me. I know he wouldn't want his parents to see it."

I said something about the legality of the situation, how I'd have to ask the chair of my department, and did he know the name of his friend's teacher so I could speak to him or her directly?

And he said, "It was you. You were Andrew's teacher."

In class, I tell my students there are words for every emotion and it's our challenge as writers to find them. I have tried over and over to explain how I felt in that moment and *every* time I fail. I can tell about the guilt, about how part of me, the idealistic part, died right then and there. I can tell you how horrible it was, but I won't even come close. "Excuse me," I said to Brian. Then I went into the office and down the hall, locked myself into a conference cubicle and cried. It was the first time I'd ever done that, and it certainly hasn't been the last.

My colleagues were really wonderful, and I might not have gotten through it without their support and advice. "Do the best you can," they told me. "Focus on the students you have now."

For me, that meant Brian.

He came to class sporadically, but when he did, he was really involved and even, I think, had a good time. He told stories about growing up on the South Side, specifically a series of instances about the Catholic school he and Andrew attended when they were kids. I don't know if it was therapeutic for him to write about Andrew, but it sure was for me to read it.

In the end, I gave him a C, and on the last day of class I asked him to stay after. "You got a C 'cause you weren't here half the time,"

I told him. "It doesn't mean you're not a good writer."

He smiled, sliding those giant headphones over his ears. "School's never been my thing," he said. "And this place costs too much anyway." He made it halfway through the door before he turned back around. "You know, Andrew told me to take your class," he said.

I waited. What I wanted to hear was, *He said you really helped him*, or *He said you were inspiring*, or *He said you almost saved him*.

What I heard instead was, "He said you were . . . interesting."

That was ten years ago. Twenty semesters. Multiply that times three classes at two schools equals—that's over *seven hundred* students I've worked with over the years, and through all of it, the names and faces and page upon page of writing, I have never once forgotten Brian.

So picture it: I'm standing in front of my faculty mailbox, getting ready to walk out the door for winter break or maybe a hell of a lot longer, and I find this book, some lit magazine from a community college, and when I open it, there's Brian's name on the top of the page. I stare at it for a while, remembering him and Andrew and how I once thought I could save the world, and then I read the story; it's about how Brian got kicked out of Catholic school for calling a nun a whore. As his mother walks him to the car, she asks, "What are you going to do with your life? What are you going to *do*?" I remember when Brian first told it, ten years ago in my class the week after his best friend's funeral—and that's when I get it: my job is not just story structure and point of view and imagery. It's Brian putting that book in my mailbox. It's Chris calling the night before he shipped out to Iraq. It's Rudy writing from prison, and Kate getting a Fulbright, and Byron starting his own magazine. I imagine a camera closing in on my face as I read that line; my eyes are wide and determined. *My God, what am I doing?* I think. *How can I give up being a teacher?*

I close the book, that lit journal from a community college, and stick it in my bag with the memos, the stack of student work.

At the very least, I'll always be interesting.

SUPER K
BY KIM MORRIS

The gun pops.

There's a split second of silence, then a chorus of heavy exhales and clicking explodes from the start line, and we're off.

I push on my right pedal, and it glides easily into rotation. I steady my left foot so that when the left pedal comes around, it'll click perfectly into the cleats on my shoe. Once I'm locked in, I settle into the saddle, and my bike and I are flying. This course is a beautifully paved road in southern Wisconsin that winds through a nature preserve. It runs over hills and through tree tunnels and spreads out gloriously into sunny stretches where the only sounds are birds chirping, the leaves in the forest shushing, and the syncopated breathing of the other racers around me. Today is a perfect summer day, eighty degrees and sunny. We take the first curve easily, snaking through it like a train, and slingshot ourselves through the next straightaway. We get ready for the first climb of the race—just a small monster, easily conquerable, but this is only the first lap. We have nineteen to go.

I am in love with bike racing, and this race is the Academy

Awards of bike racing. I've been dreaming about it for five years—since I came out to this course to support a crazy friend of mine who was like, "I'm gonna haul ass on my bike around the most gorgeous landscape in the Midwest. You should come." I did. I couldn't believe it. It was like heaven.

This is the first year my training has caught up with my dreams. I recall the long rides in April, forty miles after a full day of work, usually in the cold and many times in the rain. I remind myself that when I started racing, I couldn't even pronounce "derailleur." Now, not only can I pronounce it, I can spell it. And yet, after this first lap, there is a tiny twist of doubt in my stomach, and I can't shake the feeling that I shouldn't be here. I rest my palms on my brake hoods and take a quick look at my legs. My left calf is significantly more swollen than my right.

The swelling started when I was standing at the copier at work. The copier stopped running right in the middle of a job, so I stood in front of the machine trying to plan out my next move. That's when I felt my left calf start to swell. It was swelling, quickly, as though someone was blowing it up like a balloon. Just standing on my leg was very suddenly sending throbbing flashes of pain into my ankle. I sat down on the floor. By the time my coworker Beth found me, I had my shoe off, my pants rolled up, and I was staring at my leg, which had swollen to the point that my ankle had disappeared and my foot looked like a block of wood.

In Beth's car, on the way to the hospital, I felt my stomach sinking. "If I could just get inside my leg and take a look around," I told her, "I could just kill whatever has the audacity to show up in there, like a professional dragon fighter."

"Or," Beth said, "you could wait for an X-ray. Those do the same thing, and those don't involve you having to somehow become very small in order to jump into your own leg."

If I were a superhero, that would be my super power: jumping into people's bodies and cleaning out whatever was messing them up. I would be Super K, and my superhero power would be miniaturization. I would have a magic belt that was a whip/golden lasso combo. On it, I'd have various knives and laser guns. I could clear arteries before they closed. I could rewire the brain. I would wear a gold tiara, and in the middle of it, in diamonds, the letter K.

If you were watching this bike race from above, you'd see fifty women clumped together, rolling methodically over a ribbon of road. I've often imagined that we look like a bunch of ladybugs, glued together and hammering toward some unseen ladybug goal.

But we're not ladybugs, and there is a goal. This section of the bike race is tricky—the pavement is choppy and treacherous. The field shifts awkwardly to the left in order to avoid the wide sweep of road on the far right, so suddenly a crowd of bikes that were spread out across the road like a fan, are now in a narrow line and no one wants to be in back. I feel an elbow to my right and a leg to my left, but I need to make sure I keep my eyes in front of me because I can never remember where that huge crater of a pothole is. I think it's by that weeping willow that hangs over the road at the next bend, but I don't want to take any chances.

There is a tingling in my left calf and I can hear my doctor's haunting words in my head, but I shut the door on both of those thoughts and spot the pothole. I slide by it easily and I breathe a huge sigh of relief when I'm past it. We fly around the next bend and in the distance, we get our first sight of the real climb of this race: a six percent grade over two miles. In civilian terms? This means all muscles will be burning in a matter of seconds, an invisible vice will descend upon and quickly squeeze every lung in sight, and none of us will be able to feel our fingertips. More than likely, a significant percentage of the field will sit up here, which is the death knell in bike racing. Once you sit up, you'll never get your momentum back.

I glance ahead of me. If I can get to the top of that hill in the first couple of spots, I can nail the downhill, take the following corner by myself, and then set myself up for the hill immediately following. I see a clear line up the middle of the field, and I can't believe nobody's filled it in. I sneak slowly through the bikes, and the huffing, and the whir of spinning wheels. When I get near the front, one of the riders in a red jersey takes off and sprints for the climb. I jump with her, and in a second there's a gap between us and the field. She looks behind her, first at me, then at the field behind us, and says, "You ready?" I look down at my legs. My left is swelling more now, and I wonder if I'm gonna be able to get power out of it in a few more laps. "Let's go," I tell her.

An hour after Beth took me to the hospital, I was sitting on a bed in an exam room, my left calf smothered with gel, an ultrasound wand pressing against the exact spot that was sending razors of pain throughout my body. Glaring at me from the walls of the exam room were posters of the circulatory system, the skeletal system, a huge picture of rotting teeth with the caption, "Ignore your teeth and they'll go away."

"There it is." A friendly tech pointed to the ultrasound screen. "There's the blood clot."

"A blood clot? Aren't blood clots for old people?" I asked.

"You don't look like an old person to me," the tech said.

"I mean, I'm healthy."

The tech tapped at the ultrasound screen. "This doesn't lie."

I looked at my legs spread out in front of me. I don't know who belonged to that left one; from the knee down, the calf was swollen like a water balloon. It didn't even look like a leg. The right one, now *that* was a leg: a clearly defined ankle and a calf shaped to execute a variety of bike racing moves.

I looked at the ultrasound screen. I could see the cross section of my leg. There were bits and pieces of what looked like chalk marks along the top and bottom of the image. Every time the tech pressed the wand into my leg, the black in between the white chalk marks moved, like fresh tar. There were white wisps threaded through the black tar, except for the spot the tech motioned to. That spot was an immovable black hole. The tech pressed the wand again, the pain welled up, and I watched the white wisps and the black tar gush, moving politely around that immovable black hole.

Super K would not put up with the Blood Clot. Super K could kill anything, so the Blood Clot's days were numbered. Super K would walk into the saloon that the Blood Clot was playing poker in, and Super K would say, "Blood Clot, today is your unlucky day." The Blood Clot wouldn't look up from his cards, but the platelets would. Super K would flip the safety snaps off her laser guns strapped to her superhero belt and lightly trace her fingers along their handles. The platelets would know she meant business and scatter. "It's just you and me, Blood Clot," she'd say, and as the Blood Clot rose from the table, the brim of his cowboy hat still dipped over his eyes, Super K would whip out her guns from her holsters, spin them in her palms, shoot a staccato beat of lasers into Blood Clot's chest, and watch him blow to bits and disappear.

The field can't catch us. Halfway up the hill, my racing partner starts to falter, so I pull ahead and she drafts off me up the rest of the hill. On the backside, we scream down and fly into the next bend. I assess my options. We have a few laps left. I don't have enough energy to make that solo. I can feel that I'm starting to lose power in my left leg. My right is already compensating for it. I ignore the pain, which is like a dull throb that's about to go numb. I can see my partner is from Wisconsin. It's written on her jersey. Wisconsin bike racers are a force to be reckoned with. They climb like mountain goats, and they sprint like jet engines. It's possible this woman could blow me to dust at the line. However, I'm not going to get anywhere fast without her. We take turns pulling each other, eating up the road underneath us, putting what feels like miles between us and the field. We start to groove into a rhythm, and I can feel my body morphing with my bike. The sound of my breathing and my heartbeat and the whir of my wheels—these sounds are individual at first and as we ride, the sounds swirl out in front of me and twist around each other, and then I'm in the middle of a symphony, flying through the woods.

A week after Beth took me to the hospital, I was sitting in Dr. Clot's office. Dr. Clot is the hematologist. If he wasn't a hematologist (or, rather, if he wasn't *my* hematologist) he might be a nice guy. Amiable, laid back, quick to laugh. Still, I didn't like him, and I told him this. "Most people don't," he confided. Dr. Clot looked down at my chart. "It's called Factor V Leiden. It's a blood disorder. It's genetic. It means there isn't enough protein C in your blood. Protein C stops the clotting process. Since you don't have enough of it, your clots don't stop clotting."

"So where can I get some more protein C?" I asked. Dr. Clot didn't answer. "Nowhere? I can't get protein C anywhere? Are you kidding me? You can order humans through the Internet, and you're telling me I can't get protein C from anywhere?"

Dr. Clot took a deep breath. "I'm giving you a prescription for Lovenox. We talked about this earlier, remember?"

"Yes. Lovenox is like bionic blood thinners, right?"

"Sort of," Dr. Clot said. "And here's your prescription for the blood thinners. Start with five milligrams a day, and come in next week to get your levels checked."

"I have a race next weekend," I told him.

The silence that filled up the room was suffocating.

"The potential for head trauma as the result of a crash in a bike race is very high," he said. "The potential for head trauma, and what

I mean by that is your blood won't clot on the blood thinners, so your brain will drown, the potential for that is so exceptionally high that I would strongly encourage you to rethink your participation in next weekend's race."

"But if I don't crash, then I don't have anything to worry about, right?" I said.

"Is that realistic?" he asked.

"Yes?"

"Ultimately, I cannot tell you what to do. I can only say that head trauma is a very real concern in that scenario."

"OK, then how about I skip the blood thinners?"

He shook his head.

"So," I said. "I need to stay on the blood thinners to stop the clotting, but on blood thinners I have an increased risk of head trauma."

"If you participate in high-risk activities," Dr. Clot said. "Have you considered another sport?"

"What?"

Dr. Clot tilted his head to the side and said quietly, "I would suggest you stay on blood thinners. I would suggest you do so indefinitely."

"But . . . I'm a bike racer."

Super K would be pissed. She'd use extra bobby pins to make sure her tiara was tight on her head, and then she'd jump into her miniature fighter jet. She'd launch through the tube of the blood-clotted vein and start the search. It would be dark in the vein and every now and then a clunk sound would pop on the side of the jet. Platelets, probably. Possibly red blood cells. All known criminal associates of the Blood Clot. In seconds, Super K would have the Blood Clot in her scope. "You'll die now, Blood Clot," she'd growl, and then she'd fire. The Blood Clot would hang on to the vein wall tighter, but Super K would be undeterred. She'd flip the automatic pilot on, climb out of the cockpit, and pull herself up to the canopy. She'd pull two knives from her belt. They would gleam like stars when she pulled them out, even in the dark of this blood-soaked vein. Super K would size up the Blood Clot, and then gracefully whip one knife, then the other. They would land right in the middle of the Blood Clot, and the Blood Clot would explode. The remnants of it would be washed away in the tide of blood rushing through the vein. Super K would consider lobster for dinner.

My Wisconsin girl is revving up for a big finish. I can tell by the way she's antsy with her gearing, and she keeps moving her hands from one part of her bars to another. Brake hoods, drops. Brake hoods, drops. She's getting ready for something, so I get ready for it too. We have the last half of the course to eat up, and then we'll be in the last 500 meters, the sprint, and then the line. I glance behind me. Down the long straightaway, I can see the brightly colored jerseys of the field. They're raging over the last hill and hauling toward us. I look at Wisconsin; I watch her rear wheel. Her chain jumps one gear, then another. I snap mine to match hers and pull myself out of my saddle and pound the pedals. My right leg pushes down effortlessly, but when I go to pull up on my left leg, nothing happens. I can feel the icy lump of panic fill up my chest. I don't need to look down to know that my leg is so swollen it's about to burst. The dull throbbing I felt earlier has morphed into numbness and I suspect the only reason I don't feel enormous pain right now is because of the adrenaline. I look ahead of me. The trees are drooping over the road. Patches of sunlight sparkle between the shadows. I can't make my leg pull up on my pedal.

I sit up. I. Sit. Up. Wisconsin is sprinting ahead and in seconds, she becomes a dot in the distance. The field whooshes around me. Blinding, swirling colors: oranges; blues; purples; reds. I hear the clicking of gears and the harrumphs of riders who are just about to put everything they have into the next hundred pedal strokes. I watch them all as they fly away into the bend, and once the last rider disappears, I am suddenly alone and listening to chirping birds in the trees. I hear a muffled cheer in the distance, and I know the first rider in my race has just crossed the line. I pedal to the side of the road and work my way off the course. When I get to the curb, I take a deep breath. Then I gently unwind myself from my bike, and fade into the trees on the sidelines. ▯

AMBER
BY SAM WELLER

This is a boy meets girl story. I'm the boy; the girl is a 1980s porn queen. It's the sort of thing that could only happen to a guy who just got married. I wasn't even used to wearing a ring on my finger, and I was being tempted by the most forbidden fruit imaginable.

My new wife and I had just returned from our honeymoon in Cabo San Lucas, Mexico. When we arrived back home in Chicago, I was rested and ready to get back to work. At the time, I was a staff writer for *Newcity*. Perhaps you've seen it. It's that crepe-paper thin, alternative weekly that's distributed throughout Chicago. I know many people who have paper-trained their pets on my articles.

My first assignment after returning to work, go figure, now that I was lawfully wedded (I'll say that again: *lawfully wedded*) was to interview a porn queen. And not just any porn queen. I'm talking about Amber Lynn.

The name Amber Lynn may not mean anything to you but, if you grew up in the 1980s and remember cultural aberrations like parachute pants, leg warmers, and A Flock of Seagulls hairdos, the odds are pretty good you remember Amber Lynn.

Let's backtrack a bit. It's 1985. I'm 18 years old, fresh out of high school. I'm a scrawny, nerd of a kid with a tumbleweed tangle of blonde hair. I still have occasional acne. I don't tell many people, but I like the love songs of Bryan Adams and Rick Springfield.

It is a summer day and I'm standing at the checkout counter in a far west suburban Chicago 7-Eleven. On the counter to my right is a rectangular glass tank with sweaty hot dogs turning ever so slowly on a little stainless steel Ferris wheel contraption. Behind that, against the wall, a convenient store clerk throttles the lever on a Slurpee Machine like a fighter pilot at the controls of an F-16. The clerk is just out of high school himself, with long stringy hair coming out from under his green and red 7-Eleven visor. He has a prickly, barely grown in Chia Pet goatee, and he smells of cigarettes and deli meat. I figure that's his Chevy Camaro out there in the parking lot.

"Anything else?' he asks, in a slow stoner drawl as he hands me the Big Gulp Slurpee.

My eyes wander. I see a small magazine rack on the floor behind the clerk. Porn mags. What I would do for some porn. Don't take it wrong, it's not like I'm an addict or anything. I have a girlfriend. Renee Tripp. We do it. It's awkward. Your typical, unartful teen humping.

But porn is another matter. When you are eighteen and controlled by a physiological tsunami of hormones, you need multiple outlets.

So there I am, staring longingly at a rack of shrink-wrapped porn magazines and I'm anxious. Don't you have to be twenty-one to buy them? Or is it eighteen?

"Anything else?" he asks again with a little more force.

"Yeah . . ." I say. "Uh . . . umm . . ."

"What do you want?" he asks again. I must be interrupting his regularly scheduled bong cleaning.

My palms are layered with a film of sweat. "Uh, I'll take one of those hot dogs," I say, motioning to the rotating spit with the petrified wienies spinning round and round. God, I didn't want one of those.

It's like when you go into a drug store for condoms and buy a bunch of other shit to camouflage your real intentions: a Three Musketeers candy bar, hair gel, breath mints, computer paper, Dr. Scholl's foot spray, a pen, a Hallmark greeting card for your Mom, Q-Tips, and, oh yeah, pay no mind to that three pack of Trojan lubricated condoms.

But in this instance at the 7-Eleven, instead of rubbers, I'm attempting to buy porn, so I make the cover-up maneuver, and I order a completely inedible, undesirable, sun lamp-shriveled hot dog.

"Sure thing," the clerk says, putting on a little plastic baggie glove and grabbing a frank with his thumb and forefinger and then firmly laying the long pinkish dog inside a bun. "Is that it?" he asks, handing me my food.

I stare at the porno magazines behind him. A *Hustler* catches my attention. There's a woman on the cover, her wet lips opening up to envelop a glistening, succulent fruit.

"Yeah," I say. "I'd like a *Hustler*."

The stoner clerk just stands there and stares at me for what feels like forever.

"Are you old enough?" the guy asks, finally.

Oh my God! What does he care? The guy is barely out of high school, where all he probably studied was wood shop, and he's carding me? Get off my back, dude!

"Yeah, man. I'm 21," I say with an emphatic lie.

"Okay, dude, just had to ask," he says, picking up the shrink-wrapped copy of *Hustler* and handing it across the counter. At this point, a line has gathered and people are gawking: a housewife, a businessman, three boys buying baseball cards. They're all looking at me with my Slurpee. And my hot dog. And my *Hustler*.

I pay up and retreat.

Now at this point, perhaps you have put two and two together. The *Hustler*? Inside was a glorious pictorial of none other than Amber Lynn.

I drove home that afternoon and walked through my house, the shrink-wrapped pornographic magazine tucked firmly under my right arm. My parents were both at work. No one was home. I was alone. I bounded the stairs two at a time, went in my room, closed the door and locked it. My fingers nails clawed the plastic wrap off the *Hustler*. I opened it up and turned to the first photo spread. The woman was amazing. Tan. Fierce. Her face was framed in a tousle of teased-out big hair blond—this was the 80s, after all.

She was dressed in some sort of Victorian garb: a feather thing on her head, black corset, black lace thigh-high stockings, ankle-high black leather stiletto granny-boots. Her eyes were blue and blazing icy hot. The lips. God, the lips, they were full and wet and slathered in sex-red lipstick.

So. Fucking. Hot.

This was my introduction to Amber.

Jesus. I set the magazine down and went out into the quiet hallway. The sun was setting outside. I went to the bathroom and I retrieved an 18-ounce pump bottle of Jergens unscented lotion with aloe and lanolin. I quickly returned back to my bedroom, locked the door again, and you know what I did?

I fucked Amber Lynn.

By the mid 1980s, Amber Lynn, now officially my new girlfriend, was one of the biggest names in the porn industry. At the silken age of 19, she had already starred in 40 full-length porno films. In a year and a half, the bleached blonde bombshell had built an on-screen persona as the Joan Collins of high coitus.

So let's fast forward to 1999. I'm a journalist on my way to interview Amber Lynn. Fortunately for me, my wife is cool. *Very* cool. I just told her the truth: "Honey, I'm going to interview Amber Lynn, this porn queen who I used to masturbate to when I was younger."

"Okay honey, go ahead, have fun, be good."

My wife is awesome.

Outside the Admiral Theatre on Chicago's northwest side, it's one of those quintessential early summer evenings. The sun is setting in a watercolor blur of pinks and oranges and reds out there, somewhere over the endless sprawl of the burbs. I've parked my car and I'm walking down a leafy side street. There's a baseball game on a television set in a nearby house and the sound filters out of a screen door and onto the summer street where a small, smiling Mexican man walks by me pushing a cart loaded with warm tamales. It's perfect and it's still.

I approach the Admiral Theatre, a huge, 26,000-square-foot megaplex. It has a sex shop selling all sorts of nasty wares from raunchy videos to battery operated marital aids more suited for a shelf at the Home Depot—save for the fact that these massive drills are latex and phallic in nature.

The Admiral's really big draw is the strip show. These days, there are plenty of big-name porn stars touring the country, performing pitiable dance routines and likely getting paid massive dollars. Amber Lynn is booked for the entire week. Classic burlesque this is not.

I take a seat at a table in the center of the crowded theater. The audience is mostly post-frat, meathead white guys in between college and jobs in the financial world. They're loud and rowdy. For these dudes, life is an endless bachelor party. They bark. They pump their fists in circles. They smoke cigars. At this point, I need a drink. A waitress comes by, scantily clad, and takes my order.

"I'll have a Budweiser," I say.

"We don't sell booze," she says, looking at me like I'm an idiot. A post-frat guy at the next table over hears me order, and he laughs.

"Want an O'Doul's or a Sharp's?" the waitress asks.

Well that sucks. No alcohol. Still, shamefully, I order a Sharp's, one of those nasty non-alcoholic brews. Several strippers garbed in sequined bikinis, daisy pasties, thigh-high boots, you name it, parade by offering lap dances, but I respectfully decline. I'm here on business. I have my tape recorder. I have my pen and reporter's notebook. The venue does nothing for my arousal factor. Besides, I just got married.

I suck down at least three Sharp's before Amber Lynn takes the stage.

At thirty-four, considering her lifestyle, she looks remarkably great. She obviously works out, and she obviously has a plastic surgeon. She saunters out with the gait and swagger of John Wayne. She's wearing a pair of fuchsia-colored assless chaps and matching high heels. She's engulfed in a smelly bank of dry ice that drifts out and totally consumes me and my table and my bottle of faux-beer. I cough and wave my hand in the air to clear the fog away. The routine lasts about a half an hour and it makes the Dallas Cowboys Cheerleaders look like graduates of Juilliard. Still, it's Amber Lynn. Who cares if all she does is roll around on the floor and do pelvic grinds for thirty minutes? She's tanned, she's toned and she's that woman from that *Hustler* magazine of my pathetic youth.

Once the "dance" routine is over, I get my big chance. It's time to sit down with the "actress." She comes out from backstage—*topless*—and we take a seat at a small booth in the VIP section of the theater roped-off from the throng of horny guys circling around.

"Scoot closer to me," she says, patting the sticky vinyl booth with her long, lacquered fingernails. For those who have ever been in a seamy strip club or sex shop or an adult newsstand, you understand that stickiness. It's weird. It's inexplicable. Yet it's everywhere. When you walk, the soles of your shoes gum up and down. It's on tables. It's on the hand dryer in the bathroom. It's as if someone walked around with a misting machine and sprayed the place with I-don't-want-to-know-what. I move closer to Amber Lynn, and she nudges up next to me. I'm trying my hardest not to look at her bare tits, but then she rests one of them on my right arm. It's just this Jell-O mold, this 36D silicon can weighing up against me. I can feel her nipple rubbing up against the peach fuzz on the underside of my bicep.

The waitress delivers another faux-beer to the table.

"You drink Sharp's?" Amber says, laughing at me.

"Yeah, can't get enough of it."

The interview goes well. It lasts about forty-five minutes, her tit leaning against me the entire time. I take a different journalistic approach with her. I ask a bunch of *Tiger Beat* magazine-style questions, an ironic juxtaposition of juvenile innocence given her chosen profession.

"What's your fave food?" I ask.

"Pizza."

"Who's your fave band?"

"Aerosmith."

"Who's your dream date?"

"George Clooney."

"What's your favorite sexual position?"

"Reverse cowgirl."[1]

I turn my tape recorder off.

"You want another drink?" she asks.

"No," I say. "I've had my fill. Too bloating."

And we say goodbye. She gives me a glossy eight-by-ten photograph as accompanying art for the article I will be writing and I leave. I drive home feeling the skin on my right arm and thinking about Amber Lynn's breast rubbing up against it. It's like when Davy Jones kissed Marcia on the cheek in that episode of *The Brady Bunch*, and she didn't want to wash her face ever again.

I go home. Kiss my wife. Have a late dinner. Read. Go to bed.

The phone rings. I turn and look at the glowing red numbers on the digital alarm clock: 3:30 a.m.

"Who the hell is calling at this hour?" my wife mumbles. I leap out of bed and rush into the kitchen to pick up the telephone.

"Hello?" I answer, standing there with bed-head, wearing boxer shorts and a Social Distortion t-shirt.

"Sam?" says a raspy, deep feminine voice on the other end of the line.

"Yes?"

"This is Laura Allen."

---

[1] Sexual position. The man is on his back, while the woman straddles him, her back facing his head. She then rides him like a horse.

"Who?"

"Laura Allen," the voice says. "You know me better as 'Amber Lynn.' I need your help. I'm in trouble."

Oh God. I'm in my dark kitchen, moonlight falling in through the slats in the venetian blinds and I'm speechless. What the fuck?

Her story is absurd. She claims that the glossy glamour shot she handed me was her last, and that she makes a good portion of her income on the road by selling signed photos. The pictures fetch twenty-five dollars a pop to the horny frat boys. She claims she didn't realize that she had given me her last picture and that she needs me to come out the next night, after her routine is done, to her suite in Rosemont to give the picture back. She even asks if I can take her to a twenty-four-hour Kinko's to make copies of the picture so she has more to sell. The scenario is getting more surreal by the minute.

"If you can do this," she says, slowly, sensuously, "I'll make it worth your while."

I'll make it worth your while. The words echo in my head. What an absurd test of my scruples! I just got married and I'm given the chance to visit the object of my pubescent sex fantasies at her hotel at two in the morning? And she's going to make it "worth my while?" What to do . . . what to do?

What would you do?

I had visions of cocaine and mirrors and wah-wah guitar disco music and hour-long sloppy fellatio sessions delivered by a high porn priestess. I have to admit, it was tempting.

So I stood there and my mind raced. Stay or go? Stay or go?

In the end, hate to disappoint, I just couldn't do it. Some fantasies are better in the mind than in reality.

I often wonder what would have happened had I gone out to the Rosemont Suites. Instead, I sent a *Newcity* intern named Shane. Shane was just out of high school. Nerdy. Awkward. A face full of acne and a head of unmanageable blond hair. The kid went to the suite in Rosemont at two the next morning and helped out the porn star in distress. When I saw Shane in the office the following day, he had an ear-to-ear grin across his face like he'd just visited an X-rated *Fantasy Island* except no Mr. Rourke and no Tattoo. Just Amber fucking Lynn.

"Well," I said, "I just have one question."

"What's that?" Shane replied.

"Did she make it worth your while?"

Shane the intern was thoughtful for a long moment, relaxed like he'd just smoked a big bag of government-grade weed.

"It was a fantasy, man. A pure fantasy." And that's all he said. He walked off after that to go open mail and make coffee. ▐

A CAUTIONARY TALE?

BY ERIC CHARLES MAY

Back in the early 1980s, when I was living up in East Rogers Park, my favorite neighborhood bar was a joint called Roy's, located next door and directly around the corner from the Heartland Café. (The café's front door is on Lunt Street, while the saloon's front door opens onto Glenwood Avenue.) The bar is still there, only now it's called the Red Line Tap, in reference to the concrete wall and earthen El train embankment that sits just the other side of the narrow, southbound lane. The bar looks pretty much the same now as it did then, dark walls and ceiling and low lighting. There's still a bullet hole in the tin pressed ceiling above the bar where late on a 1970s night, a robber fired off a round from a .45 automatic to show the bartender he wasn't kidding.

So anyway, it's a warm night in Chicago, about forty minutes before last call, and the only folks in the bar are Roy, who was a stocky, long-haired Nisi with a mustache and a beer belly, me, and some white guy regular whose identity I no longer remember. These two women, who I'd never seen before, sidled through the open doorway and up to the bar. Apparently Roy hadn't seen them before either, because he immediately told them he was close to making last call. The taller of the two women said that was okay, that she and her friend just wanted to have a quick beer. This taller of the two had short dark hair and an aquiline nose with a body that was slender topside and slightly wider lower side, and dressed in an orange tank top and khaki Bermuda shorts. The white guy I can no longer remember was sitting at the end of the bar where the counter curves toward the wall, his back to the doorway. Taller woman sits down next to him, and just like that, the two begin chatting merrily away like old friends. Her buddy, perhaps suddenly feeling like the third wheel and catching sight of me sitting midway down the bar by the beer taps, picked up her brown bottle and strolled past the row of empty stools to my location. This woman was dark-haired too, but hers was shoulder-length with a sweep of it across her forehead. She was shorter than the other woman, her plump figure draped in a summer dresses, green I believe it was, that came down to nearly her ankles. When she reached me I saw she had freckles across the bridge of the sort of nose that is commonly described as pert. She gave me a cheery hello, and I said hello back. (I've always been the friendly sort. Ask anyone who knows me and they'll tell you I'll talk to just about anybody.) She asked me my name and I told her, I asked her name and she replied Mary—I forget now exactly what—Mary Pat, or Mary Kate, or Mary Ellen, one of those Irish Mary-Somethings. We began talking, and I could tell right away she was a bit tipsy: she was slurring her s's, but only slightly so. She didn't appear to be hammered. As for me, I'd had three or four beers, which, in retrospect, perhaps diminished somewhat my ability to discern the depths of inebriation in others. Or maybe she just carried her liquor well. Who knows? Of course me, being the horny young man that I was at the time, I'm thinking: "Maybe Eric get lucky tonight." Understand, I was a slender lad back then, no potbelly, no bald spot, and no gray hair. I could fit into size thirty-six pants and sometimes, not as many times as I would have liked mind you, but sometimes I did get lucky in such situations. As the saying goes, "The moonlight shines on every dog's ass every once and a while."

I asked her what she did for a living and then just let her talk about herself. By that time I'd been to the rodeo enough times to know that sometimes the best thing to do when conversing with a woman is to simply shut up. Apparently a lot of guys don't do this. Back then, whenever I kept quiet and let a woman *spiel*, the woman always appreciated it: "You're such a good listener," she'd say, and I'd think, in true horny young man fashion: *Whatever it takes darling, whatever it takes.*

So anyway, Mary-Something explained to me how she taught at a public grade school, and how she was teaching summer school because she needed the money, and how the principal of the school where she taught was a real bitch who had it in for her, but she really loved her students, and I just nodded and offered the occasional supportive comment—"Oh really?" "You don't say?" "Yes, I see why you'd be mad about that."—and resisted the urge (which is apparently natural to men) to interrupt with all sorts of suggestions as to how she might solve her problem. Because, you see, by then, I had also learned that when a woman complains to you—a man—about her job, nine times out of ten she isn't looking for a solution; she just wants to vent, which means you should just keep on shutting up, which is what I did.

As she talked on, slightly slurring her *s*'s, I checked her out surreptitiously, glancing at her body in those brief intervals when her aim of vision moved away from me. I noticed her thick ankles, which I took as a good sign because thick ankles almost always means thick calves and thick thighs, which are, of course, very good things.

Now I know what some black women are thinking: "What the hell were you doing messing with some white girl?" The fact was, I'd had a very nice black girlfriend who had broken up with me some months earlier because, as she put it: "Eric, I think you're a nice guy and all, but I just don't see where this fiction writer thing of yours is going. I mean, you don't even have a car." Which was true, I didn't have a car; not even a beat-up used one like some of my running buddies. By that summer, my college graduation was six years behind me. Sure I was teaching part-time at Columbia College Chicago and trying to finish a novel, but the exact details of my life-direction ran between vague and nonexistent, depending on what day you asked me. My ex, on the other hand, already had a master's degree and a job where she wore business suits. Understandably, she was looking for a man with a plan, or at the very least a clue, as to where he was going. Although I missed her terribly, I couldn't really blame her for giving me the heave-ho. In fact, I had been thinking about her when Mary-Something and her pal had arrived, as I had on many a night since the break-up. Was my ex was home alone or in the company of some On-His-Way-Up brother? Sitting on that bar stool, I could recall, with agonizing clarity, my ex, who was a prim and proper lady in public, and a sweaty, roly-poly potty mouth when making love. Mercy.

As for other black women, well, at the time East Rogers Park was not the hotbed of sisters that it is now, and since I didn't hang out in nightclubs, I had fewer black women opportunities, or least ways that's how it seemed to me. Of course, I also knew that my South Side female relatives were of the opinion that if I had simply chosen to live in South Shore or Hyde Park like a black man with some sense, I'd have had plenty of suitable replacements for my ex-girlfriend. But I digress.

So anyway, before you know it Roy was telling us that we have ten minutes to drink up. Mary-Something glanced over her shoulder at her friend, who was still merrily talking with that guy whose name I can't recall. Turning back to me she says: "Let's walk around the block so my friend can talk to that guy a bit more." I said sure, and off we went, Mary-Something telling her friend as we passed that we'd be right back.

We took a left out of the doorway and stepped out into the full-moon night, walking north on Glenwood, the air humming with the drone of near and distant air conditioning units. The next cross street was Greenleaf and we took a left there too, that block so heavy with trees that at night, the street light barely gets through.

Mary-Something had by then moved on to other life problems—her sick cat: "I'm so worried about Mombo. He isn't eating the way he should." Her less-than-stellar brothers: "They're just like our dad, frat-boys past their prime looking for some dunderheaded woman to momma them. Typical Irishmen." Her crummy Edgewater apartment: "There's a weird, old, Polish lady who lives on the second floor and sweeps the sidewalk in front of our building every evening whether it needs it or not. She gives me the evil eye every time she sees me. Like's she putting a curse on me. Not that I believe in that stuff."

I kept listening like I didn't have a salacious thought in the world, taking a few more clandestine glances at her not-quite toned biceps (also freckled) and her cute pudgy fingers with the short, clear nails. We took yet another left at the next corner, which put us on Greenview, and as we headed south, her right hand brushed my left wrist—once, then a second time—and I took her hand in mine and she clasped those pudgy digits through my larger ones like we'd been holding hands for months. Of course my immediate thought was: "Yes! The moonlight is shining, and the glow is pointed right at Eric's ass!" She kept talking, and soon we were at the next corner, at Greenview and Lunt, and we hung a Louie (as we used to say) east in the direction of the Heartland with Roy's just around the next corner. By then my mind was in horny-young-man overdrive; I had just a few minutes to suggest to Mary-Something, in a gentlemanly way, that she ditch her friend and accompany me to my place, which conveniently, was but a short walk through the viaduct, down a street, and around another corner.

At the intersection of Greenview and Lunt, there are large, multi-unit apartment buildings on every corner. We had just gone around the Northeast bend when Mary-Something ceased her litany of woes and said: "I gotta pee." Still holding her hand, I said that Roy's was right down the street and she could use the washroom there. That's when she took her hand from mine and said: "No. I have to pee—right now."

I glanced around: there was no else on the street; all the windows of all the surrounding apartment buildings were dark. I looked back at Mary-Something, who by then had stepped onto the narrow lawn of the building nearest us. Folks, there are those times when someone does something so unexpected, that as they begin, the only thought that runs through your head is: "No way."

Followed by, "*No way!*"

Yes way.

Mary-Something hiked up her long green dress with one hand, yanked down her underpants with the other (I remember the panties were white with a blue wildflower print), and squatted low over the grass. She kept the dress end gathered in the one hand and extended her other arm at a downward angle in front of her, the fingers spread on the ground for balance, she looking not unlike a football lineman just before the ball is snapped. Thus situated, she then proceeded to take herself "the all-time, feel-good piss," as some call it. The stream came out of her like water out a garden hose, splattering on the lawn where it collected in a pool and bubbled like a babbling brook. She kept peeing, and peeing, and peeing.

Though shocked, I remember thinking, *Boy, I guess she really did have to go.* Of course, as is always the case with horny young men, that horny side throttled on unabated. For instance, I couldn't help but note that her calves and thighs were, as I had earlier suspected, deliciously thick, the skin there far paler than that of her face and arms, almost ghostly white under the street light. Her dark pubic hair was the straight-haired kind that lies flat, as opposed to the tight curly kind. Which is just an observation, not an aesthetic judgment, since it has never made much difference to me what kind of pubic hair a woman has as long as my face is—but again I digress.

So anyway, there she was pissing like the end of a rain spout in a downpour, and I took another quick look around and there was still no one else that I could see, no late night revelers loud laughing their way home, no residents out walking the dog, no one at an apartment window or driving down the street. Finally—*finally*—she finished, and with no toilet tissue handy, she gave her hips a light wiggle to shake off the last few clinging drops. I'm now thinking that at worst, I would get out of this with a funny story to relate to my running buddies, and at best, I might still salvage the situation, and that it might be fun giving Mary-Something's nether region a gentle soap wash and rinse back at my place.

But then, alas, Mary-Something went too far.

Apparently her success at "hold up your dress, pull down your underpants and squat all in one motion while drunk" (it was only then that I realized how drunk she actually was) had given her the confidence do the far more difficult "hold-up your dress and pull *up* your underpants while rising from a squatting position while-drunk."

She did not succeed.

Halfway through her rise, she lost her balance and pitched forward, landing face bang on the sidewalk. She moaned, rolled over and slapped those pudgy fingers over her face where they stayed for a few seconds. I was bending directly over her to help when she took her hands away to reveal a nasty gash across the bridge of that pert nose. The blood gathered at the gash and then dribbled down in a thin stream over her left cheek. And all I could think was: "I'm a black man standing over a white woman at two in the morning with her underpants around her ankles, her dress up over her waist, and a bleeding face. Now is when the police will come." (And I bet there are some black women thinking: "Serve you right, too.") Yes, the police will come. And what could I have told them? What possible explanation as to my innocence could I have given, that *any* cop, regardless of color or gender, would have possibly believed? Having been raised in Chicago, I had no trouble imagining what my fate would be if the cops should happen upon me. Hell, if *I'd* been a cop and seen Mary-Something and me in that situation, *I'd* have arrested me:

"*Alright, Eric, what's going on here?*"

"*Officer Eric, this isn't what you think and I have an explanation.*"

"*Oh I just bet you do, Eric! I know all about you! Horny as the day is long!*"

"*But Officer Eric—*"

"*But me no buts. Hands behind your back, I'm putting the cuffs on you. Our mother is going to be so disappointed in you when she hears about this.*"

I looked up from poor Mary-Something and thanked my lucky stars there was still no one else in sight. I didn't know what to do first: pull up her underpants, or pull her to her feet. Then from behind me I heard a woman's voice yell: "I'm leaving!"

I turned around and there, in an orange Volkswagen Beetle parked at the intersection, was the woman Mary-Something had come to the bar with.

"Don't go!" I said urgently. "I need your help!"

Leaving the driver's door of the car standing open and the engine running, the friend got out and walked over in a huff. Though I was glad she was there, I also realized that I was now faced with the daunting task of explaining the situation to her, which my fear told me would be met with the same reaction as that of my imagined cop.

Ladies, what would *you* say if you came upon one of your female pals in Mary-Something's condition with a guy she'd met less than an hour before standing over her?

I figured she would:

a) Yell, waking up some of the nearby and heretofore sleeping neighbors,

b) Yell, and then scream for help, the scream waking up those neighbors not awakened by her yell, or

c) Yell, scream, and then come at me like a banshee with her arms pin-wheeling madly and her long, bared fingernails flashing.

But she did none of those things. Instead, she walked up and stood alongside me, put her fists on her slender hips, looked down at her bleeding, half-naked friend, shook her head ruefully, and with no request for an explanation from me, said in a voice of pissed-off resignation: "Well, let's get her up."

The friend took Mary-Something's left hand, and I took

the right. We hauled her to a standing position. "I'm sorry," Mary-Something slurred, her voice now in full drunk.

"Oh, shut up," her friend snapped. Then the friend squatted down and hiked the panties back into place while I held Mary-Something's torso to make sure she didn't fall again.

That done, the friend threw Mary-Something's left arm over the top of her back and I threw the right arm over the top of mine and we walked her to the car, Mary-Something's head lolling as she slurred, "I'm sorry, I'm sorry," the friend and me like sailors on liberty trying to evade the shore patrol and get a drunken shipmate back to the boat.

As we walked Mary around the back of the car to the front passenger's door, that little Volkswagen motor in idling chug-chug, I asked the friend: "How often does this sort of thing happen with her?" And with an angry sneer the friend said: "Frequently."

We got Mary-Something in the passenger's seat and buckled up, which was the old-fashioned, single strap across the waist kind. Her drunken body immediately slumped against the closed door. As the friend got behind the wheel, I told her thanks, to which the friend muttered irritably: "Yeah, yeah, yeah." Then she shifted the stick and drove away, leaving me in the intersection. She paused at the next cross street, which was Morse Avenue, made a hard left east and out of sight, the motor fading in the night air.

I headed back east on Lunt to Roy's, where I hoped he'd let me have a beer after closing, as he sometimes did with regulars, which would allow me to postpone my going home where I'd be alone with thoughts of what my ex-girlfriend might be doing and with whom— thoughts that were always worse in the late night than in the day. I knew Roy would be entertained by what had just happened, just as I knew that I was very lucky that Mary-Something was lucky enough to have a friend like that, and how miraculous it was that through the whole thing, no one else had come along. I also knew that my female relatives would view the night's episode as a cautionary tale for why black men like myself should confine their romantic attentions to college-educated black women who went to church.

And as I walked past the darkened Heartland Café—this was before they put a bar area in there—I felt like Paul Newman in that movie where he plays the boxer Rocky Graziano. At the picture's end he's in a motorcade because he's won the middleweight crown, and Newman looks skyward, kisses his fingertips, and says: "Somebody up there likes me."

Who knows? Perhaps somebody does. 🪑

WHY I HATE STRAWBERRIES
BY DEB R. LEWIS

At first the news that Grandpa Lewis had died struck me with the high, light tone of a steel drum. It was April 1981, I was twelve, and my first thought upon hearing that my grandfather dropped dead mowing someone's lawn was: *Now I am the only one who knows.*

We took off like it was the Granddaddy's dead Grand Prix. The whole Chicagoland Lewis branch raced down in three carloads to South Carolina for the funeral rites. When we got there, that Greenville funeral home was a hellacious circus of aunts, uncles, cousins, and who-knows-who-else, and there were kids everywhere.

What first caught my eye at the wake was an immense horseshoe wreath stabbed on an easel with the world's cheapest pink plastic phone and a pink ribbon with "God Called!" embossed in cursive gilt letters. A five-hundred-pound woman—Grandma Lewis, wife of the deceased—was destroying it so my littler cousins could call "Poppa" as he sat at the right hand of Jesus.

Uncle Leroy—hazel eyes and all—looked like someone'd slapped him silly as he strolled past, hands in his pockets, whistling. The tune might have actually been "Dixie." He leaned in to Uncle

Garrett, and announced, "Dad always said I could have that mower in the shed out back of Mama's," then continued his whistling perambulations, as if the image of his five-hundred-pound mother on all fours, cutting the grass with scissors could never trouble the clear waters of his mind.

In the front row, where Grandma should've been, creepy Aunt Rose hunched on the edge of her chair in a pigeon gray Jackie O dress, staring at the casket. I gave her a wide berth on the way up, putting my parents between me and her scary mascara eyes.

The sweet scent of lilies became so overpowering that my head was swimming by the time I stood casket-side with my folks and stared at my waxy grandfather. His hands' stillness made the burial suit look a size too big. His tongue was forever silenced, and I was relieved. His nose was a strawberry cast from Silly Putty, porous— the red drained from it in death.

Man, I hate strawberries to this fucking day. How can you eat a fruit that resembles an old man's big porey nose?

Grandpa Lewis wore long johns and overalls in the dog days of summer, with a railroad cap pulled tight over black-frame glasses and that strawberry schnozzola holding it all together. On his rare trips to Chicagoland, he'd visit a week at our house.

You'd hate strawberries too, if you were eleven and woke to his calloused hands and that big red nose pulling off your pajama bottoms, the word *no* rolling off your lips. Yeah, that *no* held as much substance as my secret transformations into Fonzie, when I'd slick my wet hair, greaser-style, and mug tough into the bathroom mirror. I said no, and he coaxed without stopping. So I watched the trains in the wallpaper pattern, where they basked in the nightlight's urine-colored radiance.

I think his glasses were off. I can tell you the sheets on the extra twin bed I was sleeping on in my brother's room had a powder-blue checked print, and that I was whispering faster than the speed of my heart as that hard, rubbery eraser of his poked around near my core.

It felt hard and spongy and my prepubescent mind leapt to . . . cap erasers. I detest cap erasers, too. Texture. With a strawberry, it's visual—though I bet the texture of an eraser ain't much different from biting into an old man's nose, give or take cartilage.

My brother, Sam, five years younger, curled like a kitten in the other twin bed far across the room, facing our shadows on the train wallpaper, sound asleep. Slept right through it.

Sam told me over the phone—once we were adults, long after I'd broken my silence at sixteen—that he dreams of waking to protect me. At the point in the dream where his rescue fails, he jerks awake, legs tight and crossed, iced with sweat. I ask if the old man's hands—busier than cobweb weaving spiders—touched him, too. Through delicate phone wires, he says no.

Back in that twin bed, grasping for safety, I wanted Sam to wake and roll over so it would stop.

I whispered, "Sam will wake up."

My grandfather said, "Shhhh."

"Mom will hear," I whispered.

And it was Saturday night, because two floors down in the living room, my parents were watching *Saturday Night Live*, which was the only thing that made anyone in our house laugh anymore. So I've got this big fucking strawberry in my face; though I don't remember his face at that point, I'm sure his nose had to be there if his eraser was poking around, trying to rub my insides out as I told him no. And two floors down—might as well been the orbit of Pluto—Mr. Bill cried, "Oh, noooo!" and my parents laughed.

I wanted Dad to come save me, and yet I would die if he witnessed me like this: in baby-doll pajamas. You know: the frilly nightie with ruffle-legged bloomers to cover your ass because the nightie's so damn short?

Only in that moment it's with the bottoms pulled off.

I couldn't tell you if he was naked or in his long johns that night, because I was riding wallpaper trains, balled into the yellow warmth of the nightlight. And that cap eraser and the lightning riding my vagal nerve—the part of you that contracts when you fall down a dark flight of stairs—that was distracting.

He heaved off to go sleep in the full bed in my room, which shared a wall with Sam's, and closed the Dutch door behind him, because the full glare of the nightlight hurt my eyes. I had to shut them. I shut down. Slept.

The morning after our *Saturday Night Live* skit, he walked me to the Bible camp bus stop. Unlike other mornings, he bought me a bag of donuts, and as we stood eating them in a cloud of powdered sugar, he said, "What we did last night? I wanted you to know what it would be like. But it has to be our secret, or you'll get us in trouble."

Well, that bag of donuts put everything on an even keel.

As for our secret, if there were a breach it wouldn't be me. I wasn't stupid. Shit, there'd been a summer visit two years prior—the week I was nine-going-on-ten. I remember: I was excited about going into double-digits. I hadn't told when he fondled me then, so why in hell would I talk about this? To his repeated whisperings, "You're number one in my book," or, "You're my eldest grandchild—you'll always be first in line with me," he added "We'll get in trouble," and "It's our secret."

I took his words at face value. I was young. Number one? I'd rather be invisible.

That was also the summer my two-year-old cousin Tammy would take off a diaper if anyone else changed her and say, "I want Poppa change me." Meaning my grandfather. It took a few years before I got the punch line.

The cloying sweet odor of lilies flooded my tongue with bile as I sat with my parents in a hardwood pew. During the funeral service in the Sistine-replica mini-chapel, the preacher waxed about how one man's life could touch so many, drawing parallels with Jesus as a fisher of men. He said, "As long you remember Joseph George Lewis—his words and his deeds—he can never truly die."

Well, I freaked. "Freaked" doesn't do it justice—I was destroyed. Through the past twenty-eight years, I can't tell you how many times that line has grated through my thoughts. "As long as you remember… he'll never die." And that twelve-year-old me? I was, like, *Remember his words and deeds? His words and deeds? Remember his deeds? And he'll never die? He'll never die!* At twelve, crying was something to be ashamed of, but I lost my shit, sobbing so hard my ribs hurt.

My mother, mistaking my sobs for grief—and God forbid someone cry at a funeral—ushered me to the ladies room, to stand with a damp paper towel on my eyes. Leaning against the vanity, Crazy Aunt Rose gave me the thousand-yard stare through three cases of mascara to ask, "You all right, kid?"

I nodded, avoiding her gaze by focusing on the cloying lily pinned to her Jackie O suit-of-the-day—navy blue this time. It rode weird because of the way her shoulders caved forward.

"He's gone to a better place," she said, her uplifted face haloed by menthol smoke. I shrugged. She zeroed on me with a tough look.

Suddenly, Mom said, "We should get back to the service, honey."

After the scoured and patriotic eulogies, the large crowd of mourners exited, leaving the family for a last mental Kodak before the coffin shut, for remembrance's sake. Well, flies remember what the spider forgets. The passage of years has clarified just how common my grandfather's secrets were. Family gossip says when my 39-year-old grandfather married her, Grandma Lewis was seventeen and pregnant with my father, eldest of eight, Joseph Junior. He's carrying the man's name; Dad's not gonna forget.

As the family filed past, Grandma Lewis sat off to the side, oblivious, playing phone with my cousin Tammy and ignoring her husband in death as much as she had in life. After she bore him eight kids, I really think she kept her mouth shut as he helped himself to my aunts—her three daughters.

Aunt Poppy, the middle daughter, stood before the casket, arms crossed, unreadable. I liked her best because she spoke to me as if was a real person, not just some kid. My whiskey-sheened Uncle Harry wandered up and belched, adding charm to his piss-darkened fly. Aunt Poppy turned, face bright as her lemon zest dress, took her brother's hand, and led him to fresh air. Years later, Dad grieved my horrid news to Harry.

Harry, in turn, asked Poppy, "Dad ever mess with you?".

"Yes, he molested me, too," Poppy'd said. "And Lana, too. And you know he got Rose . . ." She remembers, but she doesn't linger.

Aunt Lana still lived with Grandma Lewis, fetching to her calls: "Lan-ha—brang mae some tae!" Later she'd be wanted for half-baked mail fraud. "Half-baked" is a good word for Lana—I don't guess she ever went up to the casket. Probably so stoned she missed it.

And Aunt Rose: depressed, paranoid, crazy. My father blamed her Halloween birthday, but I have my suspicions. She was the oldest daughter. Like me, she was the first baby girl, only she had to navigate my grandfather every day, not just every couple years or so. She was most treasured—first in line, number one in his book, Daddy's favorite. And she kept the secret just about as well as my grandmother kept hers—except Rose's belly didn't show. Her mind broke. When Aunt Rose stood before the casket, the whispering chitchat stopped and all you could hear was the canned organ. Even her husband skulked to the back of the room. She put her hand on my grandfather's. Then she put a hand on each cheek and held him like that, longer'n you can hold your goddamn breath. The way my dad stirred, I think he felt it, too; I thought she was going to lift him from the box, and smash his head like a melon.

I looked for Grandma Lewis's reaction, but she was already out in the blinding sun.

All that was left was Aunt Rose. In the end, she bent over and kissed his forehead. When she walked down the aisle, her fingers kept twisting her wedding band. For all I know, he has never died for her—perhaps her husband lifts the hem of her nightgown with my grandfather's hands.

After Rose had gone out, Dad led the sons—Garrett, Harry, Leroy, and Milo, and the three sons-in-law—to bear the casket to the hearse. We slid into slow cars affixed with tiny orange and black flags.

Go on to the graveyard. No matter how many clods of dirt you throw down at that damn coffin, it won't cover him.

See, Grandma Lewis used to "watch" kids for people along the block. She was a foot shorter than me, outweighed me by over 200 pounds, and still had Aunt Lana fetching her sweet tea. If she could've worked it by yelling, "Lan-ha, go pee for mae," she would've. So just how close an eye did she keep—I mean, knowing the hunger her husband held for the little ones? Shit, kids were just nuts about him; my grandfather could tell whatever I yearned to hear and reflect it back from a funhouse mirror.

What I want to know is why didn't one of them speak? Flies buzz even as spider silk strangles them. Why didn't Grandma Lewis open her pie-tin face and say something? Or Rose? Or Poppy? Or Lana? What? Were their mouths too full of sugar-rolled, chocolate-dipped, short cake riding strawberries? Or maybe it was powdered-sugar donuts.

Well, choke on 'em! Choke on 'em like I do!

Fuck, forget I even mentioned him.
Forget him.
Forget'im. 🏚

FOUNDATIONALYSIS
BY LAWRENCE KERNS

"Many men go fishing all of their lives without knowing that it is not fish they are after." — Thoreau

A few summers back I came up with what I thought was a great idea—to build a full-scale replica of Thoreau's cabin . . . in our backyard . . . with my teenage kids.

I imagined us working happily together, chopping wood and hammering nails, pausing every so often to sit beneath an oak tree and read a passage from *Walden*.

As it turned out, the kids were not so enthusiastic.

Early July, when my wife and sons went away for a weekend, it seemed like a perfect opportunity for me to bond with my daughters. When I found them hanging out in the family room, Caroline, my seventeen-year-old, was sitting at the computer, checking her email the way an obsessive-compulsive checks door locks, and Gillian, my sixteen-year-old, was lying on the couch, sipping a Diet Coke and looking at *People* magazine.

So I made my pitch.

"Who wants to help me make concrete and build a foundation tomorrow?"

"Not me," said Caroline. "I'm going to Lollapalooza." Caroline talks fast, walks fast, and hates it when anything comes between her and her friends.

"No way, Caroline," Gillian said. "I need the car to go to the mall." Gillian doesn't walk if she can ride, doesn't stand if she can sit, and lying down is her favorite position of all.

I should have known that you can't ask my daughters, "Would you girls rather go to a rock concert, or mix some concrete?" If you want them to agree to help you mix concrete, you have to first propose a chore that would be much worse.

So I should have said something like: "Girls, I need you to clean up the raccoon droppings in the garage today."

Then they'd say, "Are you nuts, Dad? The boys can do that." They'll volunteer their brothers for any loathsome task.

"Sorry, but the boys will be helping me mix concrete."

"Oh, no, no—we'll help you mix the concrete. The boys can build a foundation with you anytime, but how often do they get the opportunity to clean up raccoon shit, right Gillian?"

Since the boys aren't around I just say: "Look, you girls can help me build a foundation or not, but my car isn't going anywhere until the concrete is in the ground."

Early the next morning when they shuffle out of the house, Caroline is wearing soccer shorts and flip-flops, and Gillian is still wearing her pajama pants and Sesame Street slippers.

All I say is, "Nice shoes."

"Don't start, Dad. Just tell us what you want us to do, and let's get this over with."

"Well first I want you to put these on." I hand a pair of my work boots to Gillian and her mother's rubber gardening boots to

Caroline. Then I give them each a pair of heavy-duty work gloves, and in the big boots and the oversized gloves, they look like a couple of sleepy cartoon characters.

"Now we're ready to build a foundation." Gillian rolls her eyes.

We pile some bags of Sakrete into the red wheelbarrow, and push it out to the far back corner of the yard where there's a little pond, about the size of a Dunkin' Donuts parking lot.

Next to the pond is a small clump of buckthorn and ash saplings that, ever since the kids were little, I've always called "the woods." In other words, a perfect spot to build a ten-by-fifteen-foot replica of Thoreau's cabin.

As I unravel an old vinyl garden hose, Caroline asks, "Why do you have to drag us into this, Dad?"

To tell you the truth, I don't want to drag them into it. I want them to drag themselves into it.

"I thought you'd like to walk in Thoreau's footsteps."

"I don't want to walk in anybody's footsteps. I just wanna go see Widespread Panic."

"Are you telling me you'd choose Widespread Panic over *Walden*?"

"Funny, Dad," as she checks a text message on her cell phone.

Meanwhile, Gillian flops down on a tree stump. "I don't want to stand around here all day stirring cement in a wagon when I could be shopping for a dress for Katie's wedding."

Katie is her older cousin, getting married in September on Cape Cod where their mother and I were married thirty-three years ago. Gillian loves weddings.

"It's not cement, Gillian, it's concrete. And it's not a wagon, it's a wheelbarrow. I think you girls should learn the difference."

"Why?"

"So that when your history teacher tells you the pioneers traveled west in covered wagons, you won't picture a long line of wheelbarrows with canvas tops."

You might think it's strange that I'd want my teenage daughters to learn how to make concrete. Most kids these days don't even know where concrete comes from. But that's my point; I think that knowing where concrete comes from is like knowing where babies come from. It's just something these girls should know before they leave home.

Within an hour, Caroline's face is streaked with dirt and perspiration. Gillian is sitting down again, checking for chips in her purple nail polish. In all fairness to them, it's hard work mixing concrete. And bonding with your father.

"You know what? You girls are gonna thank me for this some day."

"Thank you? We're not even gonna forgive you."

Eventually, we establish a rhythm: I turn over a lump of the mix, Gillian adds water, and Caroline rakes it back and forth until it's smooth. It feels good to be making concrete with my daughters.

But then I have to go and open my big mouth, "Hey, this isn't so bad, is it?"

Gillian says, "I'm not gonna lie to you, Dad. It definitely *is* that bad."

Why do my kids have to be so honest? Why not lie to me? I remember when I used to lie to my grandfather pretty much on a weekly basis. He was ninety-two years old, and every Saturday morning he'd put on his green overalls, get his wooden toolbox with the rickety handle, and go out back to work on his garden gate.

My mother would send me over to help him and he'd say, "Are you sure you don't have something better to do, young fella?"

So I'd lie. "No way, Pa. I wanna help you fix that gate." That's all I want from my kids: a little harmless deception.

Then Caroline lifts a shovelful of the wet mix and announces, "We're not like you, Dad."

Now just for the record, I don't want my kids to be like me. I want them to have skills I never had, to read philosophers I never read, to be creative in ways that I never was. In other words, I want them to be better than me.

So I add a little more water to the mix and say, "Just out of curiosity, in what way do you think you're not like me?"

"For one thing, we don't care whether it's a wheelbarrow or a wagon."

Whereupon Gillian adds: "And we don't like mixing cement all day either."

"Listen girls, we're not just mixing cement. We're building a foundation."

Caroline is now holding the hose in one hand and the hoe in the other. "I just want to hang out with my friends."

"You hang out with your friends all the time."

"No, I don't. I never get to do things with my friends. Because you always want us doing things with you: practicing golf; reading *Walden*; building a cabin."

Gillian sits down again. "She's right, Dad you want to be together with us too much."

I'm flabbergasted. "There's no such thing as being together with your daughters too much."

Gillian is unmoved. "Spending your whole weekend mixing cement with your father is too much. It's unnatural."

"It's not unnatural, it's . . . poignant."

That's all I was trying to do: create a little poignancy.

One after another we poured sixty-pound bags of concrete mix into the wheelbarrow, mixed it with water, and poured the sludge into the four-foot deep cavities in the earth.

By the time we pour the last of the concrete into the ground, the sun is ready to set. I'm exhausted and relieved but, as I'm rinsing off the shovel, Caroline points at the foundation and shouts, "Oh my God, Dad, look!"

Swimming in the pool of slush, struggling desperately to get out, is a little frog, about an inch long with brown spots on his back.

I pluck him out, and as he wiggles in my hand, Caroline rinses him off. Then he jumps down and hops back towards the pond.

My first thought: *Whew! Thank God a frog didn't have to die for my cabin.* But then Gillian says, "Oh, no—there are more."

I look down into the hole and now there are frogs everywhere. They're popping out of little burrows, falling into the pool of concrete, and swimming for their lives.

My next thought: *If I have to get all these frogs out of there, it will ruin everything.*

As I'm debating the issue in my own mind, I hear my daughters scream, "Save them, Dad, save the frogs! You have to save them!"

I drop to the ground, plunge my hand into the concrete slush, and begin scooping out frogs by the handful. Caroline rinses them off with the hose and Gillian makes lots of sympathetic noise.

One by one, we liberate the frogs from their concrete grave, and they hop off giddy toward the nearby pond. In the process, however, we're making a gigantic mess and destroying our new foundation.

When the last frog was finally saved that day, I stood up, brushed myself off, and looked at my two daughters standing there. With their waterlogged boots and concrete crumbs in their hair, they looked soggy. And they looked muddy.

But for the first time all day, they looked happy. 🏛

XENA: CARDBOARD PRINCESS
BY SARA KERASTAS

The first time I saw it, my face froze just inches from the screen. I'd bent over to turn on the cable box in my parents' TV room, and when I rose—there it was, this slow crane-shot descending on two sleeping women in the forest. One of them was a brunette tiger of a woman wearing a leather bodice, and the other was this tiny blonde in a tunic. They were spooning on a bearskin rug.

Cut.

The closing credits appeared on the screen for *Xena: Warrior Princess*, and my 17-year-old ass was still bent over and stoned from the contact high of what I'd just seen. In my chest was something I'd felt only three times before. The three times my friend Lisa had kissed me on the cheek: after school that one time, smoking pot in her Toyota Rav4, and once when we drank too much of her mom's Kahlúa and she put me to bed on her couch.

Lisa.

Lisa listened to Tori Amos on vinyl. I did almost anything she said.

I glanced up quickly and looked around, then noted the details: 11 a.m.; Saturday morning; WGN channel nine.

It was the north suburbs of Chicago, the summer between my junior and senior year of high school. I had just been fired from the Love's Yogurt on Skokie Boulevard.

The next Saturday at 11 a.m., I sat on the couch, gripping the remote while keeping an eye on the entrance to the room. Over the next hour, I discovered that *Xena: Warrior Princess* was a sloppy mix of grade school Renaissance Fair and Lifetime made-for-TV movie. But. There was a scene—this time in the middle of the episode—where Xena and her blonde sidekick Gabrielle were riding bareback through the forest on a horse. The week after that, Xena had to suck the poison out of an arrow wound on Gabrielle's chest. The week after that, my sister Jenny walked in midway through the episode.

"Ew, are you watching *Xena: Warrior Princess*?"

"No . . . I'm . . . just flipping through the channels—surfing."

Thank God my thumb had hit the back button and saved me. Animal Planet appeared on the screen.

"Okaaaaay." She drew out the word suspiciously. "Can I watch with you?"

"Nah, I'd rather be alone," I sputtered with forced indifference.

Jenny looked at me crooked, like a puppy hearing a foreign noise. She knew something was up. Jenny is three years younger than me, and we've always been similar—same zodiac sign, same walk, same affinity for roughhousing. Our older brother was always telling me to stop telling Jenny what to do, but I didn't. I swear. She just copied me.

"Why can't I watch TV with you?"

"I just want to watch alone, okay?!" The tension was getting to me. Every second that Jenny stood there was another second of missed Xena.

"Sara?! C'mon, just let me watch Animal Planet!"

"I'm not watching Animal Planet! I told you, I'm flipping through the channels, okay? Can't I do that alone? *God.*"

Jenny looked at me for a beat, let out an angry breath, and

plopped herself down on the opposite end of our L-shaped couch. I stared at her in disbelief. She stared at the TV. We were both wearing baggy pants, but mine were vintage sailor jeans and hers were Adidas warm-ups from soccer practice. Sometimes her ability to fit in really pissed me off. The slow British wildlife narration slid through the air, accentuating every second. Maybe Xena and Gabrielle were taking a dip in a pond together right about now. Maybe they were hand-feeding each other venison and mead at a local inn. *Maybe* they were traveling through a dream world after Gabrielle's evil daughter killed Xena's centaur son, and they were belting their emotions into each other's eyes through song! I threw the remote control on the carpet and stormed out of the room.

Later that week, I was sitting in the kitchen by the family computer, this old Gateway PC with dial-up Internet, and Lisa and I were talking on the phone.

Lisa.

Lisa had one of those Winona Ryder pixie cuts that changed colors every couple weeks. She also stuck a big orchid in the side of her hair—the perfect blend of sophistication and punk.

"Sara, you're coming over to my place," she demanded in that alpha hot girl kind of way. "C'mon, I wanna hang out! We can, like, watch a movie or something and drink my mom's Kahlúa." We did this a lot. 'Cause this is what you do with your close friends in high school, right? And Lisa and I were close, right?

"Oh, yeah?" I said, trying to sound sharp and cool like her. That was something I'd noticed recently: when I was around Lisa, I talked the same way she did.

"Yeah. Aaron's gonna come over, too."

Lisa had just started hooking up with this guy Aaron, who was like twenty years old with white people dreads. To me, he was a walking, talking, hemp-pants-wearing cockblock. But Lisa loved him. Suddenly, hanging out with her meant hanging out with him, too.

"Oh, God. I totally wanna come over," I started, scrambling for a way out, "But I'm, uh, busy tonight. I'm hanging out with some people or whatever."

After we hung up, I sat there staring at the computer blankly. I noticed that the Netscape Navigator search bar was open. I typed in *Xena: Warrior Princess*, and five zillion Xena sites popped up.

Immediately, I opened another window—a non-Xena one, so if anyone walked by, I'd have a cover-up just a click away. And then:

*Click—the official *Xena: Warrior Princess* website.

*Click—Maria's Xena Fan Page.

*Click—Xena-and-Gabrielle-Forever-Lovers-Eternal.org?

It was like giving a kid chocolate for the first time. I couldn't get enough.

On the TV show, Xena and Gabrielle were more than just friends: they were soul mates. On the Internet, I discovered that Xena and Gabrielle were more than just soul mates: they had raunchy warrior sex. They were corporate bigwigs in modern day Miami. They headlined any fantasy that any leztastic superfan could think up.

Late at night, when I was sure no one was around, I would descend into the kitchen, dial up, and stay on those websites until three or four in the morning. Most of the "fan-fiction" followed a similar story pattern: the Xena and Gabrielle-type characters meet, they fall for one another but do not share their feelings, they hold back until they can't restrain themselves any more, they profess their love for one another, they have raunchy warrior sex, and from this point on, they never hold back. The computer screen was often the last light on in the house, its neon blue glow illuminating my face while darkness cloaked me from behind.

It was around this time when I noticed that Jenny had started watching the show. I walked into the front TV room one Saturday morning and—"Oh, hey, Jenny. I need to watch something. What are you watching right now?"

"Xena."

"What?"

"Xena: Warrior Princess. I don't know. It's a good show."

"What?! Hah. No, it's not." It was a knee-jerk reaction. Protection.

"Shut up! I like it!"

"Uh, that show is a total piece of shit. I can't believe you're actually watching it! Like, seriously!"

"Shut up. I just like it. I think it's good."

Her eyes returned to the screen and stayed there. I let out a couple shocked guffaws, but she didn't budge. There was something immediately threatening about the whole thing, like if Jenny watched the show, she would see the lesbian subtext—especially in seasons three and four, I mean, come *on*—and then she'd find out why I was watching the show. It wasn't a fear of coming out; it was a fear of something deeper. It seems so obvious to me now, but back then, at seventeen, I was overweight, and subconsciously, that had taken a toll. Someone like me was not supposed to be sexual, much less sappy-lesbian-warrior-sexual. Who did I think I was? People would make fun of *that*. And that was something I was not going to risk. I started turning the whole thing into a big joke. And I was relentless.

"Hey Jenny, maybe you should check if *Xena* is on."

"Shut up."

"Hey Jenny, I bet they make Dungeons & Dragons cards with Xena on them."

"SHUT UP."

"Hey Jenny, I just saw this gross forty-year-old guy with a mullet wearing a Xena t-shirt—"

"*Shut up, Sara!*"

When Jenny went to camp in Wisconsin for two weeks, I thought it would be funny to buy a life-size *Xena: Warrior Princess* cardboard cutout for her return.

The cardboard Xena stood over six feet tall in this intimidating yet sexy pose, carrying her chakram in one hand and a sword in the other. I propped her up next to me as my mom and I waited in this parking lot for Jenny's camp bus to arrive. My mom had watched me fold Xena into the car, obscuring the rearview mirror, but she hadn't really picked up on what was going on.

"Are you sure Jenny's gonna like this, Sara?"

When the bus finally rolled in, Jenny was one of the first to come bounding out of it. I could barely suppress my giggle, when I saw her scan the parking lot and spot us about fifty feet to the left. A look of pure fear took over her face.

"Welcome back, Jenny!" we yelled.

"Oh, my God. Oh, my God. No. What is this?!"

"We got you Xena! She's super excited to see you!" I gloated, suddenly feeling a weird mixture of uncomfortable feelings as her tears of embarrassment welled.

"I can't believe you fucking did this, Sara." Jenny dropped her pack, hurried into the car, and slammed the door. I really hadn't anticipated her being this upset about the Xena cutout. *Wait,* I thought, *was she watching the show for the same reason I did?*

My mom stood in the background as her confused arms sank to her sides.

At home, my mom told me to put Xena away, so I carried her upstairs to the attic and awkwardly ran into Jenny on my way.

"Sorry," I said. "I thought you'd think it was funny."

She barreled past me, her shoulders knocking Xena and me into the railing. I reset my grip, continued up the stairs, and slid Xena behind a dresser in the attic, which was perhaps not the most thought-out storage spot, because a week later, Lisa spotted it.

Lisa.

We were in the attic smoking cigarettes out the window, so my parents wouldn't smell. Aaron was on tour with his band that week, so suddenly we could hang out one-on-one again.

"*Whoa.* What the fuck is that?" Lisa blurted out of nowhere.

She was straddling the windowsill. With her vintage green dress draped over the edge, she looked like one of those French cigarette ads from the 1940s. I wanted to tell her I'd missed her, but I held it back. There was a moment of silence, and I realized she was waiting for my response. I quickly followed her eyes to see Xena's intimidating yet sexy smirk peeking out from behind the dresser. Shit.

"Oh. Ha! That's just a Xena cardboard cutout my sister got," I said nervously. I knew Lisa didn't know about my Xena stuff— there was no way she could—but these very separate worlds were too close to each other, and my hands started to sweat.

"Oh. My. God. This is a joke." Lisa flicked her cig away, then pulled Xena out from behind the dresser. "Sara! We have to do something with her! We have to, like, take her out somewhere."

"Wait, what?" I rattled my brain for any available excuse. "I don't know, it's my sister's, I don't think she'll want—"

"Come on. She won't even know. We'll take her to Dominick's or Dunkin' Donuts or something, and bring her right back. I promise. It'll be so fuckin' funny."

So.

We drove around Evanston, Illinois, in Lisa's Toyota RAV4 with Xena sitting in the back seat. We pulled into an empty Dominick's parking lot, hot-boxed the RAV4, and blew smoke in Xena's face. Hot-boxing, for the record, is when you're in a small space—usually a bathroom or a car—and you seal all the openings to the space: windows, doors, cracks underneath the doors. Then, you smoke pot. If you're in a bathroom, you turn on the shower to get some steam going. The idea is that you create a space with as little fresh air as possible, so that the THC is recycled over and over again. One person's exhale is another person's inhale. It's one of those stupid things you do when you're seventeen on a Friday night and have nothing to do. Oh, and it gets you extremely high.

When we finally opened the doors to the RAV4, I imagined large gusts of pot smoke flying past my ears and floating into the night sky.

It was a summer night montage: parading ourselves into Dominick's, passing Xena back and forth like a flag. The store was empty at 10 p.m. on a Friday, and the momentum carried Lisa and me in different directions.

I was standing alone, mesmerized by this rainbow wall of chips, when I sensed someone else was there behind me. I glanced to the right and saw Xena's head, peeking out from the end of the aisle. Then, like some sort of battle charge, Xena started coming at me full force. She was getting closer and closer, tilting to the left then to the right, faster and faster, but never changing her expression. I could barely react before she smashed right into me, the cardboard bending over my head as I crumpled to the floor.

"Oh, my God, Sara! You should've seen your face!" Lisa spat out between gasps for air. I could feel her spasms of laughter through the cardboard, and I started to laugh too, but I wasn't laughing the same way. Mine was mixed, a release of too many heightened emotions. Xena's head was bent over my right shoulder, Lisa's over my left. These worlds collided. Her orchid smell mixed in with the dust of ripped cardboard. This was the closest I'd ever been to Lisa, and this moment was everything: ecstasy, release and embodiment. No holding back of anything. Just long enough for me to feel connected. Then it was over.

"Oh, shit!" Lisa laughed. "Your sister's gonna be *pissed*."

She rolled off of me, and held up a portion of Xena's disembodied shoulder in front of my face.

"Oh . . . no, that's okay. I don't even think Jenny—" I trailed off.

Xena's chakram was missing, her neck torn at an unnatural angle, and there were scuffs everywhere. I looked up at Lisa, searching for anything to indicate that she'd just felt something, too.

"Whatever," I said.

We lifted Xena and carried her outside like some sort of funeral procession. The tiny rectangular opening of the Dominick's garbage bin wouldn't accept even one of her gargantuan thighs, so we had to rip her up. First at the knees, then at the waist, then the neck.

Getting back into Lisa's car, the stale smell of smoke and weed awaited us. I sniffed my t-shirt. I didn't want to smell like that. Lisa got a call from Aaron, and put the car phone on speaker. On the way home, it was hard to tune out their conversation. I wanted Lisa to drive faster. I stared out the open window, trying to disconnect. To cut off everything in the car. I peered out into the deep darkness, and wondered if this was all there was.

THE KIDS AND THE KING
BY KHANISHA FOSTER

Andre is tiny for a fifth-grader. He keeps looking out the side of his headtto see what he can get away with. His teacher, Miss Ortiz, pointed him out to me on the first day. "He's a non-reader," she'd said, while over her left shoulder, Andre had thrown a lightning-fast punch into his buddy's right deltoid. "Don't expect him to be acting. He won't be able to memorize lines."

I'm an arts integrator in the Chicago Public Schools, fusing the teacher's curriculum and my art form—theater. My job is to make learning and text three-dimensional for the students. Touchable.

The classroom started as a perfectly structured space with each desk placed in a measured straight row, but now that I'm working in it, it looks like that scene from Fantasia where Mickey is playing wizard for the day.

Miss Ortiz's hips negotiate the crooked aisles between the desks. She's a walking fertility goddess. Most of the kids listen to her like she's their momma. She lifts her eyebrow and the whole class goes from Fantasia to military school. She is centered grace; I am perky, jumping around the room, turning chairs upside down and asking students to find meaning in it. Andre is not shy about telling me how ridiculous I look. "Not to worry," I tell him. "You'll get used to it."

The black kids think I'm Latina. I can tell from the half-hearted *holas*. The Mexican kids think I'm Puerto Rican, and the Puerto Rican kids think I'm Mexican. Their heads tilt trying to figure out the structure of my voice. It clips up at the end, as if everything is good news, and the sounds push through my nose like I have a cold.

Miss Ortiz twists her long black hair around her hand and throws it behind her. "I wanna do a project on the civil rights movement for MLK Day," she says. "Do you think we could tie literacy goals into that?"

Fireworks go off inside my body. She has handed me my dream unit! She can't tell by the lightness of my skin or my thin floppy hair, but I am the daughter of a Black Panther father who married my Irish-German mother; together they created a kid full of cultural pride and extreme curiosity. My bookshelves at home are stacked sideways with books about the Civil Rights Movement, the Harlem Renaissance, the history of racial integration in New Orleans.

The mecca of them all, my favorite book, sits alone on my coffee table: *Freedom: A Photographic History of the African-American Struggle*, by Manning Marable, Leith Mulling, and Sophie Spencer Wood. I spent months looking for this book, not sure that it existed at all. "I'm looking for a photographic history of the Civil Rights Movement," I'd said to numerous bookstore clerks. "Something that has different images from the same three pictures we see every February. You know, MLK at the podium, Rosa Parks in her horn-rimmed glasses and, if we're getting really risky, Malcolm X in his bow tie."

"Not that those are bad pictures," I would add, careful not to offend. "It's just that, isn't there more?"

I was searching for the story behind those three pictures. Books line my shelves because, even as an adult, I can't imagine how these three frozen moments, alone, changed America. Where is the rest of the story? Who aren't we hearing from? My father talks to me about sitting in a pew at Emmitt Till's funeral, and watching the Chicago Police Department surround the building where hours earlier they had shot and killed Fred Hampton—events I didn't see in any of my textbooks or hear about from any of my teachers.

But what I'm really curious about is why my father turns into the Incredible Hulk when people cut him off in traffic, or why the n-word shoots out of his mouth when he would never let me use it, and why his eyes always look so hurt.

In our packed Chicago classroom, the kids are recreating three pictures I've given them from the book. There's an eleven-year-old, cornrowed Billie Holiday crooning in the corner, there's a group of boys—no taller than five feet—holding marker-drawn signs that say "I AM A MAN," and a little girl holding her textbook to her chest surrounded by a frozen jeering crowd; instead of the starched flat-ironed top worn by the little girl from the Little Rock Nine, our student wears a Baby Phat jacket.

A quiet boy named Marcus sits cross-legged at his desk, holding *Freedom* in his lap. He pushes the book up for the class to see, cutting me off as he says, "Hey y'all, look at this! Martin Luther King is small, and he look like he's country."

The students break out of their statues and run over to the picture, pushing each other along the way.

"Dang Andre," Little Billie shouts. "He's as small as you are."

"Shut up!" he shouts, cocking a fist and popping his chest real fast in little Billie's direction.

"Hey," Miss Ortiz jerks, whipping a right up sheet into the air, "Andre, you want another one of these?"

"No," he grunts. "Sorry. Dang."

Marcus and the others flip through the pictures. I'm nervous they'll rip the pages. They stop on a picture of Jesse Jackson pointing to the sky.

"What's this one?" Marcus asks, bouncing around in his seat.

"That is . . ." I start, slowing my words long enough to figure out how to phrase this for a class of fifth-graders. "That is a picture of . . . well you guys know that Martin Luther King was assassinated."

Andre makes a gun out of his fingers and points it at his buddy with the bruised arm.

"Clip-clip-bang-bang you're dead!" he gloats. His buddy maneuvers a fake machine gun across the room. *Teta-tet-tet! Teta-tet-tet!* The boys instantaneously drop to the floor, dying graphic fake deaths, and the girls double over with laughter, clapping their hands together with screams of glee at every shot. My eyes meet Miss Ortiz's in horror across the room. Her eyebrow is not working. I start waving my arms in the air.

"OK, stop!" I say, trying to hide the squeaky panic in my voice. "No weapons!"

The lifeless bodies start to jump up from the floor.

"Oooohhhh. Who gets to play the assassin?"

"I want to be it!"

"No, me! Me!"

"Do we get guns? Do we get to use guns?"

The boys are falling all over each other with excitement. Andre plants his hand on his buddy's face and pushes it to the ground. "I'm playing the assassin."

His battle cry silences the class. I look at Miss Ortiz, and she looks at me. Even a momentary pause in a fifth-grade classroom could mean the end of the lesson, so I jump in.

"Okay wait . . . hold on guys . . . sit up . . . Andre get off of Paul. If—if—we choose to write a scene about the day that Martin Luther King died, we are not going to write a scene that glorifies the person that took his life."

They're staring at me blankly. I am re-thinking the word "glorify." "Okay, look," I start, lowering myself like I'm defusing a hostage situation. "Violence"—I say the word before I know what I am going to say about it—"violence is hard to talk about. Especially when we're discussing a time when so many senseless acts were happening. Acts that made it seem like violence was the only answer, but we are going to talk about it."

How are we going to talk about it? I wonder. I don't tell them about my real experience with violence. That at five years old I'd found a gun in my father's black duffle bag, and when I'd asked him why he had it, my tiny hands shaking, he only said "To protect myself," with that sadness in his eyes again. And I don't tell them that the violence of that time had led my father to heroin addiction, to stealing, and giving up, to unremembered moments of violence against my mother. To prison. Moments that lived in his blackouts and in my memory. Moments that I thought about every time I made a decision.

Instead I say, breathless on the inside but somehow stable on the outside, "Martin Luther King spoke about fighting back with love and peace, one person at a time. So, I'm going to ask you: how do we fight back against the thing that we hate the most without turning into it?" The students aren't completely with me, but they aren't shooting fake guns at each other anymore either, and I take this as a good sign.

"I tell you what, guys. If you want to write about Martin Luther King we can, but it's got to be about his message and not his killer. You have to try to answer that question."

I make it through the class, barely, and when I get home that night I collapse into my bed with my *Freedom* book, flipping through the pictures and wondering if the people in them would be proud of how I handled myself today, or if they'd knock me upside my head.

My cell phone rings. Andre's mom. "I wanna talk to you about this business of Andre playing the man who killed Martin Luther King," she says. "That's my baby up there, and if you think—"

I cut her off in my "good daughter" voice. "No ma'am. First of all, I appreciate you calling. He is not playing the man who assassinated Martin Luther King. I would never allow that." My voice is sounding more like my white mother's than my black father's and I'm wondering: Is that a problem? "We're going to honor him. We will not be acting out his death—"

"I should hope not," she says, returning my respectful cutoff. "I don't send my son to school to glorify the killer of an American hero. I'm gonna be at that performance, and I better not see anything I don't like."

"Agreed. Agreed." I'm nodding even though she can't see me over the phone, and she's gone.

In class the next week, Marcus is shy with pride. "We voted, and I get to be Martin Luther King." He smiles.

Andre's body is flipping around in his seat. "What about me? What do I get to be?" He pushes the words through his teeth.

I pull out the book. "Well it's a bit early to start assigning parts," I say pushing the desks aside and pulling the chairs into a circle. "We don't even know what we're writing about yet."

"Yeah we do!" Little Billie Holiday shouts as she grabs the shoulders of her classmates, pushing them into their seats. "We're writing about MLK, and about how he didn't want people to fight, and about how all men are created equal."

"True," I say, folding my legs up into my seat and opening the book. "But let's fill in some gaps." I flip through slowly so the whole class can see the pictures. "Stop me when you see something you want to know more about."

I flip past a picture of a former slave with a railroad track of scars running every which way across his back and another of kids their age working in a field, but they call "Stop!" on a picture of a group of black people dressed to the nines, corsets and all, from the late 1800s. Marcus's lips curl into a smile. Andre's nose circles around his face trying to figure out the picture.

"What's that?" he asks.

"Well," I explain, "These are students in the science laboratory

THE KIDS AND THE KING

of the Tuskegee Institute. Here are the Fisk Jubilee singers touring London to raise money for the college."

Andre walks up real close to the book and turns the pages without asking, almost like he's searching for something.

Over the next few weeks we put what we learn from the book into our bodies, creating tableaux. In so many of their recreations, mouths are open. The work is done in silence, there is no actual sound in the room, but it's as if you can see their voices shouting, singing, and preaching, and everyone is somehow listening. The frozen moments of black history grow into scenes about teenage girls being arrested after a peaceful protest, and the imagined dialogue of President Roosevelt's black cabinet. The students are particularly struck by a picture of Emmitt Till's mother falling to her knees at her little boy's funeral, her exhausted body being held up by those behind her. They all want to be in this one, and they line up behind the frozen pictures of his mother speaking the words that they may have said had they been there themselves. They decide the final moments of our show should be Martin Luther King's words, and not his death.

On the day of the performance, my students swarm around me in panic. "Marcus isn't here," Little Billie reports. She's the stage manager. My right hand.

"What do you mean?" I ask. "Is he sick?"

"No. He got suspended yesterday. He hit Paul and busted his lip."

I bury my head in my hands as quickly as I raise it out again. My Martin Luther King just got suspended because he beat somebody up. I look at Little Billie. "All right, can we get a copy of the script? Can somebody read it?"

"We don't have to. Andre's got it memorized." I look past her to the stage where Andre, in a three-button charcoal suit, is highlighted by midnight blue curtains as he does a mic check.

Billie continues her report. "The parents are being seated—we saved you a seat in the front—the designers are backstage, and the actors are in the wings . . ." She lifts up the word "wings," proud that she's speaking theater lingo. "We are starting in five. Do you want to say anything to the group?"

I can barely get out a "yes" past my smile. She pulls me behind the closed curtain, and the glow of their faces warms the stage. "You have taken words off the page and made them live," I say, catching a lump in my throat and pressing it down, strangely careful not to show too much emotion to a group of kids who have shown me nothing but. "Thank you for answering questions that I could not answer myself."

As the curtain opens, Andre's mom is sitting directly behind me. I feel her adjust around shoulders to see the stage better. The students' frozen bodies, filled with pride and knowledge, embody these forgotten pictures on the stage. They show us the music of Holiday, the protests of children, the loss of innocents, and the responsibility of hate. The text grows from them as it did in our classroom, but they speak like experts now. The audience stills. Andre steps forward. I grab the wooden arm of my chair, nervous that he hasn't had any time to rehearse.

"Darkness cannot drive out darkness," he begins, and I swear I am hearing Dr. King himself. "Only light can do that." He raises his open palm into the air. "Hate cannot drive out hate." The words rumble from his belly. "Only love can do that." The audience starts rocking forward and back in their seats, putting their hands into the air, nodding. Andre breathes them in and speaks the final words of Reverend Martin Luther King's speech from the night before he died: "I have seen the Promised Land, and I may not get there with you, but I want you to know tonight, that we, as a people, will get to the Promised Land. So I am happy tonight. I am not worried about anything. I am not fearing any man."

And with that, nearly overcome by the power of King's words becoming his own, Andre falls away from the microphone into his friend's arms, just as MLK had. His mother shoots up in applause behind me and the rest of the audience follows. Over their clapping and cheering, I ask Andre's mom. "Did we make you proud?"

Andre's mother wipes the tears from her cheek. And she nods.

HOLLYWEIRD
BY JC AEVALIOTIS

I had told myself I would never walk in there. No matter how badly I needed a job, I found it comforting to think that there were still things I wouldn't do.

So I prowled Hollywood, first hitting the nicer restaurants and bars in Los Feliz, then heading farther and farther west. Down Hollywood. Down Sunset. Past the homeless drug addicts dressed like superheroes posing in tourists' photos outside of Graumann's Chinese Theatre. Past people hocking celebrity death tours. Past teenage hustlers posing for men old enough to be their grandfathers. Bars. Coffee shops. Restaurants. Nobody was hiring.

I was twenty-four and broke. I had been in L.A. for a little over a month, just another miserable stereotype grinding it out in paradise. And despite all that you see walking around Hollywood, the strangest part of my day was walking home past the Scientology Celebrity Center, just a block from my apartment. It was a seven-story Hollywood fantasy-castle hallucination. Formerly called Château Élysée, it used to be a resort for the big stars during Hollywood's golden age. Scientology acquired it in the 1970s; in the

'90s they restored it, creating the perfect Hollywood incongruity. This mirage towered over the vacant lots and slums of Hollywood, the weirdest part of a weird landscape. There was a massive green neon Scientology sign perfectly positioned to command the 101. At street level, there was a big sign that read, "Now hiring." And every time I passed, I would think, *No freakin' way.*

Scientology is one of the biggest landowners in the city, so you see their buildings all the time. And more likely than not, you know someone who's become a Scientologist and had their career take off. Or their lives ruined. Scientology in L.A. is like a microcosm of religion in our country: divisive and ever-present and something about which everyone has an opinion.

One night, walking home with my roommate, we passed by the Celebrity Center. He pointed out the "Now hiring" sign, a banner flapping in the wind, and made a joke about me working there. I laughed with him about it, but I stared at the Scientology sign for a long moment that night before closing my curtains. Rent was due in ten days, and my money was gone. That night passed slowly, light from green neon a block away seeping in through the curtained window.

The next morning I donned khakis and a button-down. I put a few resumes into a folder and walked to the Celebrity Center.

I'd expected something creepy and cult-like, but the lobby was just a lobby. It was a place Errol Flynn had visited in the '30s, and it retained some faint residue of Hollywood glamour—Deco and tasteful with a polished hardwood front desk.

I approached the desk. "I saw the sign out front and I'm wondering what kind of jobs—"

"Just fill this out," said a woman even more polished and beautiful than the lobby. Her olive skin and almond-shaped dark eyes were framed by jet-black hair in twin braids. She didn't wear make-up; she didn't have to. She also didn't have to waste time on a guy like me, so she handed me a stack of papers with the barest moment of eye contact.

"This is the application?"

She nodded and smiled, showing a row of perfect white teeth.

"But, but what kind of job am I applying for?"

Her smile hardened, something flinty underneath it. "Just fill it out, then we'll see what you're suited to do after the orientation."

The phone rang, and she waved me away.

I took the application and settled into a plush mid-century armchair. I started flipping through the ten-page application. The first page or so was normal stuff: name, address, education, job history. But then we got into red-flag territory.

They wanted to know my social security number and my medical condition. They wanted to know if I was taking any prescription drugs. They wanted to know if anyone in my family had a history of conflict with Scientology. They wanted to know if I was there gathering information for a news story. They wanted to me to summarize my current debts: how much I owed and to whom I owed it.

There was a logo for something called "The Sea Organization" on the front page. I knew I should get out of there, but I needed work. I desperately needed to work. I sat there, pen hovering over the application, when a man in a suit approached my chair. He was in his twenties, with underwear model features, wearing a suit tailored closely around an obviously perfect body. *Where the hell do they get these people?* I thought.

"Sir, you're here for the orientation." It wasn't a question.

"Actually, I just looked through the application and—"

"Don't worry about the application, you can finish that after the slideshow."

I paused. A Scientology slideshow?

Without really thinking about it, I stood up to follow the guy. I didn't know whether I was curious or desperate or weak-willed. Maybe all three.

The guy in the suit moved quickly, not looking back and not talking. We walked down long corridors, then through fire doors and down flights of stairs. Closed doors labeled only by numbers. Pictures of L. Ron Hubbard on bare plaster.

We went down another flight of stairs. My palms were starting to feel sweaty, and I realized there was no way that I could find my way out on my own.

Finally, we stopped at a door with a wooden table next to it. I leaned down to look at a stack of blank documents on the table. The guy in the suit put his hand on the small of my back politely pushed me into the room, pulling the door shut behind me. I had just been shut underground in the Scientology castle, shoved into some dungeon. I wondered why the suit didn't want me to see the documents outside the door. I noticed my heart beating faster and I tried to remember if I'd told my roommate where I was going.

It was a small, shabby conference room. A carousel slide projector stood on a rickety table and cheap-looking wall sconces provided dim light. Metal folding chairs faced a projector screen. Nothing about the room matched the opulence or perfection or menace upstairs. It was a broken-down little basement conference room. There were other people there, more than five but fewer than ten. Roughly my age, dressed to look for work. A few looked weirded out. Most avoided eye contact. Who were these people? Just looking for a job, maybe behind on their rent? Was this also the very last thing they thought they'd do? Were they scared, too, or was it just me? *This is how they get you,* I thought. Then I took a seat in the world's weirdest waiting room and wondered what they were going to try to persuade me to do and whether I would have the strength to say no.

The door opened and a dumpy-looking kid no older than twenty-one entered. He wore wrinkled black slacks and a baggy white shirt with a black tie. He didn't walk so much as slouch forward. He fit this room perfectly, the office coordinator behind the curtain in this Scientology Oz.

"Morning, everyone," he said. "My name is Ethan, and I'm here to welcome you to the Scientology Celebrity Center."

He continued. "L. Ron Hubbard once said, 'The world is carried on the backs of a desperate few.'" Ethan paused, taking a rehearsed look around the room, letting it sink in. "Unfortunately, it is these few who are often the most neglected. It is for this reason that L. Ron Hubbard saw to the formation of a special Church of Scientology, which would cater to these individuals—the artists, politicians, leaders of industry, sports figures and anyone with the power and vision to create a better world. That's the mission of Celebrity Center, where you sit right now."

He looked up. No one said anything. Ethan cleared his throat and went on, talking about what Scientology had done for the world and L.A. In the '70s, Hollywood was a dump—dirty and dangerous.

"But now," Ethan said, "Things are better. You know how all the benches at bus stops have partitions that keep bums from sleeping on them? Scientology did that."

As Ethan spoke, I felt my fear evaporating. His pitch was ridiculous. The poor guy was terrified.

Ethan went on. "Before I talk more about the present opportunity, I want to tell you more about L. Ron Hubbard and his technology." Then he dimmed the lights. I leaned forward in my seat, ready for the hard sell. Ethan fumbled with the remote. Then the slideshow started: blank screen, low rumbling soundtrack, then a shot of Earth from space. Gravelly voice says, "The world is beset by wars, plagues, and addiction." Under this, slides of burning cities, crying babies, a junkie shooting up with a hypodermic. Long pause. Voice brightens: "The only hope for humanity and the planet is L. Ron Hubbard and his technology, Dianetics." On screen, a portrait of L. Ron, pasty-faced and gray haired and fat.

We learn about L. Ron's service in World War II, as a naval officer. In 1950, done with the Navy, he went on a spiritual and scientific quest to gain knowledge to better humanity. He spent a series of years on yachts researching and writing the books that would become Dianetics, pivotal to the founding of Scientology. And a group called The Sea Organization was composed of Scientology's most committed, working at the front lines. The slide show wrapped up with pictures of all the people Scientology had helped. The final image was Tom Cruise, hollow-eyed and manic.

Ethan brought up the lights, glanced at his notes and tried to bring it home. Sea Org was like Peace Corps for Scientology, a place where young idealists give three years working for something bigger than themselves. Sea Org's structures were based loosely on the Navy because L. Ron's service was so important to him. And because he wrote *Dianetics* on a boat.

He threw out lingo: "Operating Thetan" and "Clear," which was the state inhabited by luminaries like Tom Cruise and John Travolta. All I had to do was sign on for a three-year stint and my room, board, and expenses would be provided. I would work to help spread L. Ron Hubbard's technology, and, best of all, I would receive free course-work and auditing, the process by which Scientologists pursue spiritual advancement.

Ethan stammered on. Despite the astonishing inanity falling, haltingly, from his mouth, I felt sorry for him. He could've been me weeks or months ago. Broke and desperate and lonely. This was the secret to the Scientology? The pathetic pitching to the desperate?

I was no longer scared or amused or curious. I was angry. At L.A. At my joblessness. At myself for not knowing what the hell I wanted. At Ethan and the half-dozen of us scraped from the bottom of the barrel.

I raised my hand and said, "Ethan, can I ask a question?"

The others in the room shifted in their seats.

He licked his lips and said, "Um, yes, go ahead."

"So I came here to apply for a job and instead I've been subjected to this hour-long pitch to join this religion. Is my employment here contingent on becoming a Scientologist?"

Ethan rubbed the back of his neck. Finally, after an awkward moment, Ethan responded, "If you're in Sea Org, you get to take the classes for free." Then he looked at me, half-smiling like we were on the same team now.

"I understand that, Ethan, but that's not my question. Can I work here without taking the classes?"

Ethan just looked at me, mouth agape. "But, the classes are free . . . John Travolta . . ."

"OK, Ethan, thanks. I'm done here."

Then Ethan looked really nervous. He put down his papers looked me straight in the eyes. "I'm afraid I have to ask you to stay until the presentation is over, sir," his voice quavering as he spoke, his posture stiff and unnatural.

I laughed aloud. Ethan looked as if he'd been struck.

The others in the room looked anywhere but at me. Ethan started to talk again. I cut him off, "Ethan, you're not actually suggesting that I'm not free to leave, are you?"

Ethan blinked. He opened his mouth to speak, then shut it. He sighed. "No, of course not, sir. You're free to leave. Scientology hopes you have a nice day."

Ethan told me that someone would accompany me to the nearest exit.

The others in the room looked relieved when I stepped into the empty hallway. I noticed the table again. Before I could think about it, I reached out and grabbed one of the documents, slipping it into my folder. The guy in the suit came around the corner. "So you won't be joining us today?" he asked, looking at me like a disappointed big brother.

"Nope," I said, "I need to pay rent, not change religions."

He looked like he wanted to say something, but he set his jaw and turned to lead me out. Every step I took closer to the surface made me more relieved. It also made Ethan and the suit and the beautiful woman behind the counter seem more and more absurd. I might've been poor and desperate, but at least I wasn't a sucker.

Eventually we got to ground level again, the sun shining into the lobby. The suit walked me to the door, and held it open for me. I stepped through then he stepped out behind me, standing squarely in the entrance watching me. I walked through the exquisite garden and to the wrought-iron fence. I turned back. The suit was still there, still watching me.

I opened the gate and stepped back into the manic desperation of Hollywood. I looked around, the sunlight bright after my hour underground. I opened my folder and pulled out the Scientology contract. It was a legal-sized document, on expensive heavy stock and embossed with the logos of Scientology and Sea Org. At the top, it said "Sea Organization Religious Commitment." It was a really basic contract:

I, _____

DO HEREBY AGREE to the religious commitment of membership in the SEA ORGANIZATION, and, dedicate myself to achieving the goal shared by Sea Org members, which is to bring about spiritual freedom of all beings through the application of LRH's technology.

Being of sound mind, I do fully realize and agree to abide by the purpose shared by Sea Org members which is to get ETHICS IN on this PLANET AND THE UNIVERSE and fully and without reservation, subscribe to Sea Organization discipline, mores and conditions and pledge to abide by them.

THEREFORE, I COMMIT MYSELF TO THE SEA ORGANIZATION FOR THE NEXT BILLION YEARS. (As per Flag Order 232).

There were spaces for the new recruit to sign, then spaces for witnesses and for the recruiter who performs the "Sea Org Swearing In Ceremony."

I stood in the street, blinking in the hazy sunlight. Then I read it again: a *billion* years.

I was still broke and unemployed. But I felt better than I had all week. I put the contract away and headed west down Hollywood. Maybe there were a few restaurants I hadn't hit yet.

DIRTY DANCING
BY BYRON FLITSCH

For those of you that don't know: gays have holidays. You know, Jews have Hanukkah, the straights get Super Bowl Sunday, and us Chicago gays have Pride Parade in June and, in August, Market Days. It's pretty much a huge drunken street fair in Chicago's Boystown neighborhood, and it usually involves major kick-ass parties at people's homes where there's free booze, loud music, and a naked shower contest.

Did I just say, "Naked shower contest?"

Let me start from the beginning.

It was one of those humid Midwestern summer nights. I was twenty, walking down a busy sidewalk, dodging people walking dogs and couples holding hands, cell phone to my ear, and suddenly, my mom says:

"Your Aunt says her friends saw you at a gay bar. Are you . . . gay?"

My stomach drops. Bam. Right there on the sidewalk, my life changes.

I lie at first. "Um . . . well, uh . . . of course not! I have gay friends and we like to go out!" but then I realize it's now or never. I stop walking and take a deep breath.

"Yes. Yes, mom. I'm gay."

There are instant tears from us both, then she hangs up on me and won't answer phone calls. The next day, my parents drove to my studio apartment in Chicago—as a surprise—thinking I needed to see a shrink to "fix the issue" and, when I say, "I don't have an issue. The issue might be yours," my mom stormed out of my apartment. My dad shook his head. And as I closed the door behind them, my mom yelled, "You are not my son anymore."

She meant it. For five whole months I was disowned.

Wah wah wah. I *know*. This is pretty tame for a coming-out story, I realize that now, but this story isn't about coming out. It's about how, when my parents disowned me at twenty, I went broke.

Very broke.

I was a college student at art school when I was outed, working a part-time job, going to summer school, and eating cheese sandwiches 'cause that was all I could afford. My parents had been paying half my rent so, for those five months, I had to do . . . *things* to make-up that extra cash. I had do . . . things that haunt me to this day: sold the watch my grandpa left me, eBayed a pair of Helmut Lang jeans, and—something I never imagined I'd do.

Get that shocked look of your face! This is not a prostitute story!

Though it does involve getting naked.

It's August of 2003, two months after the whole outing incident. I'm dating this guy we will call "Jerk," who, though he was making enough money to help me out financially, decided that his habits of smoking, drinking, and buying Diesel jeans suited him better than helping me. All my money that summer went to finishing the tuition tab I rang up at summer school. I tried to pick up more hours at my part-time job, but they didn't have much. I tried taking on another job, but I was starting school in a month, and no one wanted to hire someone who barely had time.

Which brings me to the shower contest.

Jerk invited me to a party, and let me tell you, this was not just some thrown-together affair. All the neighbors combined porches in their back alley; every single staircase led to a different party. Picture it: there were giant curtains closing off the party at the entryway. Then, as you walked in to the courtyard off the back alley, there were large spot lights screwed in to the walls. Attendees were all the rich gays sporting tucked-in polos and expensive sunglasses—doctors and lawyers in the same couple!

I was *super*-intimidated.

"I need a drink. Bad," I said to Jerk.

"God, you're high-maintenance," he replied, rolling his eyes and heading off to the bar. We'd only been dating for a few months at this time, and—I'll admit—I was pretty naïve. I let him talk to me that way because I liked sleeping in his air-conditioned bedroom. I was too broke to have air conditioning.

I used a man for air conditioning.

He comes back with a clear plastic cup. In between the loud beats of techno dance music pounding out of the giant speakers, he yelled, "I signed you up to be in a shower contest."

Most of you know what these are, sort of. At least you know the hetero version of them: wet t-shirt contests. You know, contestants stand in the middle of a pool, and then water shoots out of a hose, and people cheer as you see people's nipples get hard through tight white shirts. In the gay world, we do this with tight white underwear.

"I'm not doing that!" I yelled back over the beats, taking a panicked swig of what I think was vodka and orange soda.

"Well, you can win money, and I'm tired of hearing how broke you are."

And with that, he recognized a friend and disappeared. As I stood looking through the messes of beautiful people all sweaty from the humid August weather, all tan from the summer sun, all drunk from the flowing booze, I realized I had two options:

1) Escape. Give up and move home and tell my parents I'll change. I could even marry a nice girl. Right?

2) I could figure out a way to get money that wouldn't involve a shower.

In the end, I chose a third option: get drunk and see what happens.

Growing up, I was a good kid. I was in 4-H, you know, the farmer's club? I was a Cub Scout! I was on the honor roll!—*good kid*—and I knew that dancing in a shower for money was not one of those things you do as a good kid trying to grow into a good adult.

But when you hate your parents for pretending you don't exist, when you're dating a guy who's a lot older for his AC, when you're desperate to show everyone that you're able to take care of yourself—when you're *twenty!*—you do things. Maybe things that involve showers.

Not gonna lie: I drank a *lot*, probably more than I'd ever drunk in my life.

And then it began.

They pulled all the stops out for this contest. There was a microphone. A popular drag queen was the host—she looked like Tyra Banks in a bikini, and I remember asking myself, and maybe strangers, where she was tucking her junk in something that tiny. The shower was set up on the third floor of a balcony. I remember this because I counted the steps to remember where I was and, when I got to the twentieth, I realized I had been duped. See, the other guys that were going to dance were *professionals*, either real-life strippers or porn stars. They had muscles you find on the covers of *Men's Fitness* and they were wearing tight white underwear that . . . you know. They were . . . *taut*.

"I can turn around. I can turn around. I can turn around." I remember repeating to myself, but it was too late. A giant floodlight lit the balcony, and finally I got a good look. On the center of the balcony was a giant pink kiddie pool, you know, those plastic ones people have for kids in their backyard, and hanging from the balcony rafter was a hose with a watering spout that was shooting water. There was a DJ spinning records to the left, and to the right, Tyra stood with her microphone, looking over the balcony at hundreds of horny people ready to see what me and these five hot porn stars had gotten ourselves in to.

"Okay, lovers! Let's get this party *started*!" she screamed. "Rules are, you dance in your underwear *for the entire song*! See this jar! It has three hundred dollars in it! And whoever we think gets wet best wins it!" She lifted the glass jar. The light hit it just right, I could see Benjamin Franklin's eyes meet mine, and I swear he winked. I swear he was saying, "Just do it, Byron! You're going to be rolling in me later!"

I was wasted.

The competition was talking to each other like they've been best friends forever. One could even flex his ass muscle.

The music started—Cher, naturally—and the first guy gets in the pool and shakes his stuff. Water drips down his back, soaking his entire body. Tyra smacks his butt, and the crowd goes insane. He danced to the entire song. It was disgusting.

And beautiful.

The next guy, a studly blonde wearing boxer briefs, did this incredible booty shake thing. The guy after him was even better—dark black hair. Italian, I think—and the guy after him was just gorgeous. *Gorgeous.* He danced to the George Michael song "Freedom," and the way that he moved his body with the water looked like a high fashion cologne ad. The wetness glistened down his chest and the floodlight made his muscles pulsate. You could smell the hormonal musk of the crowd.

And then, of course, it was my turn.

I knew I had to step it up a notch if I wanted win that money. I knew that being a skinny vegetarian with only slight muscle definition wasn't going to get the crowd. I knew that I had to do one thing that would make them remember me, scream for me, vote for me. Guys, all I wanted was that money.

And so, when my song came on, I made the executive decision to go for it all.

It's still pretty blurry: I stepped into the lukewarm kiddie pool; the shower turned on and it was pretty damn cold since it was coming from an outside hose; the DJ played the dirtiest rap song, "My Neck, My Back" by Khia, which had slutty lyrics and a sultry beat—perfect for what I was about to do.

I took my shirt off and let the water soak my face and hair and chest. Then I took my shorts off. I had on cute Calvin Klein black boxer briefs. I kicked the water. I bumped my ass to the beat. I shook my head. I heard Tyra scream in delight. I heard someone in the crowd yell, "More!" and then I took my underwear off.

There I was: completely naked and dancing. While cupping my balls.

That's when I see them: flashes.

No. Not the cops.

It was worse: *camera* flashes.

People were taking pictures of me.

I sobered up. Like, *immediately*. I realized what I was doing. Nude. For money. But still, I couldn't give up. I cupped. I danced. I finished—and just like that, it was done. The spotlight went out, the music quit, and the crowd went back to their drinks. "When do we find out the winner?" I asked Tyra, dripping wet and barely dressed.

She stroked my face with her press-on nails. "Oh honey," she said. "You're adorable."

This was the night I discovered how awful people can be. Jerk had left for some bar and hadn't even seen me dance. Someone printed those pictures of me in a local gay rag. And worst of all: the money was a joke. No one was ever going to win anything. It took me two days to get over the hangover, and years to forgive myself for taking part in something so degrading.

In the end, people forgot about the pictures. I forgot about Jerk. And a few months later, my parents apologized for how they'd reacted. All that's left is getting through it: sometimes you're proud, sometimes embarrassed, and sometimes you learn something you'll never forget.

Like how to cup your balls while dancing in a public shower.

RUNNING ON EMPTY

BY JULIA BORCHERTS

The minute I pushed open the glass door of that ghetto gas station, baby on my hip, I realized that the clerk had been shot. He wasn't behind the counter on the left; no, he was splayed across the back wall as though he'd tried to make a break for it, blood pooling through the two holes under the patch that said "Kevin" on his blue uniform shirt, one mangled and bloody hand stretched out in front of him, as though he'd been pleading for mercy or trying to block the final shot that pierced the front of his skull and blew out the back of his head. Bits of his long, light-brown hair hung from the chunks of blood and bone smeared along the wall where he'd hit and then slid down. He'd been a tall man, I noticed, because his legs, positioned awkwardly akimbo in ways that would have been too painful to maintain if he'd been alive, had knocked over a display of motor oil three feet to the right. He was a young man, too, I realized, probably younger than I was then, which was twenty-three.

I froze in the doorway, ten dollars clutched in my hand, until my daughter wiggled on my hip.

"Bottle," she demanded punching me on the shoulder. That, not mama, had been her first word, and she used it often. It was 8 p.m., and she should have eaten an hour ago, but we'd run out of gas and had to trudge through a blizzard in this bombed-out stretch of neighborhood on the west side of Rockford, Illinois.

"Bebop, be quiet. We'll be home soon," I lied, sliding my own back away from the glass front of the building and across to a rack of roadmaps. I didn't know whether to bend down and try to get a pulse or go back out into the dark, and I kept asking myself, *What would my mother do?* But she was way too competent for something like this to happen to, and this was exactly the kind of situation that made her judge me as inept. There was a pay phone across the lot, but I hadn't seen or heard anyone screeching out into the street, and I'd been staring at the gas station for half a mile as we walked down Auburn Street, willing it not to close before we got there. This meant, to me, that the perpetrator could still be skulking around the building, and if I tried to use the phone, my back would be exposed.

There'd been a series of killings that week, and I knew as soon as I saw this gas station clerk slumped on the floor that I'd walked into another one by the same guy. The day before, an attendant at the Citgo gas station up the street had been murdered, and the day before that, two clerks at Willie Fredd's corner grocery store had each been shot in the head five times. Later that week, two shoppers would be gunned down at a Radio Shack in Beloit, Wisconsin.

By the next week, we would learn that the killer's name was Ray Lee Stewart. His own father would turn him in for the reward money, Stewart would get the death penalty and, in 1996, he would be executed.

But that night in January of 1981, I didn't know any of this. All I knew was that I was trapped in a gas station with a dead body and a nine-month-old baby. I shivered as she squirmed in my arms. She reached over my shoulder with her fat little hand, and I felt the wisps of her hair, light-brown and fine like those on the dead man, brush against my cheek as she grabbed a road map and threw it across the room, where it hit the open cash register. The window rattled as the freezing rain hit the glass, and I realized that I could stay in there all night, but aside from the weather, we weren't any safer inside than we were out in the parking lot, and that sooner or later, someone would show up, and at this point, I'd rather it was the police. So I pulled Bebop around to the front of my chest, pushed the door open and staggered back out into the snow.

So, you might be asking, what the hell kind of mother takes her kid out in a blizzard, during a killing spree, in a car with no gas and doesn't even bring a bottle? The easy answer is that my husband and I had separated a week earlier, and I was exhausted from shuttling my kid between babysitters while I worked two jobs. I was taking my work clothes and a load of shitty diapers to the laundromat, and I had no idea how I was going to make the house payment, let alone fix the broken gas gauge on the car.

But the true answer is that I really wasn't ready to be a mother. I was twenty-one when I discovered I was four months pregnant, and while that may not seem criminally young, it had taken me four months to discover this because my husband Greg, a lazy but patient roofer with spiky, dark hair who moonlighted as a drug mule for the Hells Angels, was bringing home so much speed that I hadn't gotten my periods for almost a year. I had stopped speaking to my mother after I overheard her telling Greg to keep an eye on me because I wasn't dumb, exactly; I just had no common sense.

But it was too late for a legal abortion, and even as self-absorbed as I was, it occurred to me that there was no good reason for a married couple, even Greg and me, to give up their kid for adoption. To my credit, I did give up drinking and drugs and signed up for Lamaze classes as soon as I got the news, but I spent most of the pregnancy smearing my belly with cocoa butter and examining my hips for stretch marks. All I cared about was when I could start drinking again and how I was going to get my figure back. Greg responded to my badgering about how we were going to afford this baby by picking up roofing jobs in southern Illinois, where it was warmer, making additional runs for the Hells Angels, and smoking a lot of weed.

But since he was now gone approximately all the time, and I was stone cold sober and getting fatter by the minute, we did nothing but fight. By the time I was seven months pregnant, I was sick of waddling around with a forty-inch belly, and he was sick of hearing me complain about how the baby bruised the inside of my ribs and smashed my internal organs flat with her kicking. But still, that was no reason for him to out me to the Lamaze instructor, Martha, a fidgety redheaded nurse in her mid-thirties with plastic glasses and three chins, who was also a rabid fan of breastfeeding.

"Does anyone have questions?" she'd asked the eight couples assembled around the long, Formica-topped table with the "Breast is Best" signs hovering over us. I wanted to stab Greg in the neck when he raised his hand.

"My wife drinks a six-pack of Coke a day and now the baby has hiccups," he told everyone, ignoring my kick on his shin. "And I think that all that caffeine is probably making it nervous and all that carbonation is probably giving it gas."

He had a point, but I wasn't about to admit this in front of Martha, or the other couples, all of whom were at least ten years older than me and whom I'd overheard gossiping about my smoking. I was a little ashamed that they'd pegged me as trailer trash, but I quietly judged them too, and their eagerness to join the club of dull moms whose conversation revolved around the feeding, sleeping, and pooing habits of their kids. I was only twenty-two by then, and I'd decided that I wasn't going to change anything about myself just because I was about to be a mother and that I would never, *ever* use the phrase "going down" to refer to my kid's nap rather than my husband's activity around my vagina.

"You *jerk!*" I snarled, but Greg pretended not to hear. How dare he complain about me when he's out snorting coke with the Hells Angels?

All of Martha's chins began to wobble as she nodded at me. "You should give up cola now," she said. "You certainly won't want that in your system when you're breastfeeding."

I was debating whether or not to ask Martha if that would be better or worse than the kid getting a contact buzz from its dad's rampant weed-smoking when Greg popped in with, "Well, she's not breastfeeding. She wants to wear a bikini this summer and she's afraid it will ruin her tits."

Martha began zipping and unzipping her sweater as the other couples collectively swiveled. "I can't believe you don't realize how much more nutritious mother's milk is for the baby than"—she paused for emphasis—"*canned* formula."

"She eats Doritos for breakfast," Greg continued, glaring at me, his dark eyes narrowing. "I don't think that's so healthy for the baby."

A nebbishy, henpecked dad-to-be from the other end of the table started waving his hand in the air. "And she smokes!" he yelled.

Martha made eye contact with everyone in the group except for me. "Well, maybe," she said, "In *this* case, formula might be a better choice." It was, I am sure, the first and last time she ever made that statement.

So I was going to get to keep my tits, but as Martha moved on to the next question, I saw the other parents sneaking sidelong glances at me, and I knew they already felt sorry for my kid.

I wondered, a week after Bebop was born, what Martha and those other couples would say if they'd seen me almost drop her on her head at three in the morning when I fell asleep on the couch while feeding her a bottle of, yes, formula. And I thought about them again and how they'd judge me the night that my husband and I split up.

Greg had just gotten home from Mexico, where he'd brought back something like ten kilograms of heroin, most of which was shoved into our freezer. He'd smoked a joint while I unpacked his suitcase and we'd gone to bed at ten, but I'd had to get up at midnight with Bebop, who was nine months old by then and teething. I was crabby because it was my mother's birthday, and I'd been too stubborn to call her, and I was exhausted because while Greg enjoyed playing with Bebop and never lost his temper with her, he was the kind of dad who passed her right back to me as soon as she got fussy. I gave her a teething biscuit to gnaw on, but she just kept whining, so I finally rubbed some Jack Daniel's onto her gums, poured a few shots for myself and brought her into bed with us. I passed out and didn't feel her climbing up onto my back like a little possum, where she fell asleep, too. Everything was fine until I rolled over and Bebop flew off my back, screaming through the air till she hit the wood floor.

She was fine, it turned out, as she always was, despite me. But Greg, who wasn't happy about being woken up, started yelling.

"I'm afraid to leave town half the time," he said, stomping in his boxer shorts to the bathroom for a glass of water. "Because I never know what'll happen to my kid if I'm not there to watch you."

I cuddled Bebop into my chest and kissed her sore head. "You think I'm a bad mother?"

"Look, even your own mother thinks you could use some help."

I jumped off the bed. "You talked to my *mother* behind my back?"

"She only wants to help," he said quietly, running his hands through his short, spiked hair.

"*You* don't help me," I yelled.

"I'm out trying to make money," he said. "And I never wanted kids. And you're the mother. It's your responsibility, not mine."

That did it.

"You know what?" I started, "I want a divorce." I stomped into Bebop's room to put her in her crib, and it broke my heart when I realized that she was safer alone in her own bed than she was with me.

He slept on the couch that night, and when I got home from work the next day, his clothes were gone. He called a few days later to give me his new phone number, but by then, I'd gone out and gotten a second job. He said that he missed Bebop but that he couldn't take her with him, since he was always leaving town for work. I didn't answer the phone for a week, afraid that if I picked up, it would be my mom or Greg. I was trying to prove that I didn't need anyone's help, but I realized that snowy night on the way to the laundromat, even before I ran out of gas, but around the time I discovered I'd forgotten Bebop's bottle, that I was failing.

The wind was still blowing sideways at thirty miles per hour, and I could feel, through the back of my coat and the scarf I'd wrapped around my face, that the temperature had plunged below zero, but the snow, at least, was starting to let up. I made it to the pay phone without incident and managed to call 911. Then I swallowed my pride and made a quick second phone call to my estranged husband. Fortunately, he answered on the second ring.

I took a deep breath and then burst out with, "I can't talk because I just discovered a murder, and the killer might still be here, but I need you to pick up Bebop and me at the Clark gas station at Auburn and Kilburn right now."

I heard an exasperated sigh. "Christ, Julia, what the fuck is wrong with you?"

I wanted to slam down the phone, but I didn't have anyone else to call.

"Can you please just come?" I pleaded. "The car's out of gas and the police are on the way, but I don't want to walk home with the baby in this blizzard."

My kid had commenced to howling, and the only food options at the gas station involved a couple of vending machines—one for cups of pop and coffee, the other for snacks. Bebop didn't have too many teeth yet, so, true to my white trash roots, I bought her a Hostess Twinkie for dinner, which at least seemed less likely to choke her than a candy bar or chips.

She was contentedly gumming her Twinkie when a dozen squad cars careened into the parking lot, sirens blaring, lights flashing, the first set of cops leaping out and running into the gas station without even slamming their doors.

The detective arrived at the same time as my husband, who snatched Bebop out of my arms, his spiky hair quivering with aggravation. I snatched her back, handed him my keys and asked him to go get her car seat so that the police I was getting to know wouldn't feel compelled to arrest us for illegally transporting the kid on my lap.

The snow had stopped completely, but the temperature had plunged to twenty below zero by the time the detective finished asking me questions and Greg got back. Shivering, we strapped Bebop into the back seat, and she fell asleep as soon as he started the car, which is when I started crying. It was 1 a.m., and I was going to have to get up at 5 a.m. to get to work. I was also going to have to wear a dirty, frozen uniform to my second job as a waitress, because the laundry baskets were in the trunk of my car and the laundromats had closed while I was busy running out of gas.

"Do you think," I sniffled, as we pulled out of the parking lot behind a patrol car that was cruising slowly down the street, "That we could come home with you instead?"

"You've had a rough night," he sympathized, his dark eyes softening as he put his arm across the back of the long bench seat.

"Maybe if you were around a little more, we could have worked this out," I suggested, unbuckling my seat belt to scoot closer to him.

He retracted his arm. "You should have thought of this before you told me to leave."

"Maybe I made a mistake," I offered, and reached for his hand.

He pulled off onto a residential street and we sat and watched a few squad cars circle around the block while Bebop snored in the back seat, snuffling through what sounded like a dream.

Finally, he let go of my hand and leaned back against his window, shaking his head.

"This sounds like an attempt at regeneration," he said. "And if we learned one thing from zombie movies and Stephen King novels, it's that regeneration is not a good thing."

I know I shouldn't have done what I did next, but I was

desperate. I leaned over to put my arms around him, thinking that maybe if we started kissing, I could talk him into taking us home with him, at least until I could figure out what else to do. But he saw it coming and pushed me away with both hands.

"Don't," he said, but he said it with some sadness. "It's too late for that."

And I realized then that he was through with me. But I was going home to an empty house on a freezing January night with a serial killer on the loose. And goddamn it, I was only twenty-three years old. If I was going to get through this and not fuck up completely, I needed help. I turned to my soon-to-be-ex-husband.

"I want my mom," I said.

He nodded his head and shifted the car into gear. And as new snow started falling quietly around us, he drove me home, to my mother's house. 🏠

TRIBES
BY CP CHANG

According to the influential, highly respected, and (dare I say) groundbreaking blog, *Stuffwhitepeoplelike.com*, multiracial, multi-cultural couples are in. So my black girlfriend, Jess, and I, a Chinese man, are theoretically hot.

Jess is hot by herself. She has this thousand-watt smile that brightens a bad day; she's funny, kind, a brilliant writer, and always has intriguing things to say about art and film and books and race and culture. In fact, talking about race and culture is how we met: I saw her at a reading when she spoke about being overseas, in southwest England, where she was the only black woman for miles around, surrounded by people who spoke the same language as hers and yet immediately saw her as a stranger. I said to myself, "I've got to meet this woman: she gets exactly where I'm coming from, even though I'm not exactly a black woman in England."

All of this makes it ironic that we've been fighting about race and culture. Take this past December. Jess and I had been dating for about a year and a half, and we had moved in together in October, but this was the first Christmas we had spent together. We went to

Danville, Illinois, to spend the holiday with Jess's grandmother and her extended family. Danville, if you haven't been there, is this flat, small city, bracketed by a thin river and train tracks, with dozens of mom-and-pop stores. It's the kind of town where smokestacks and pickup trucks are the most common sights. There were sixteen of us invited to Christmas dinner, and Jess's grandmother only has this little ranch house that's just enough for her and her dog.

Jess's extended family was eager to meet me, the first guy she's ever brought home for the holidays. I had already met her parents, and while they were perfectly nice to me, I knew that I, as the man living in sin with their daughter, had some work cut out for me. I hoped to get in good with the extended family.

As soon as I got through the door, Uncle Derek hitched up his pants, hoisted himself off the recliner, and gave me the two-handed handshake—you know, the one that says, "Everything is cool, but I'm the uncle you gotta answer to." Uncle David, short and stocky, smiled while he sat me down for a friendly interroga—uh, chat. And a cousin who played linebacker for the Fighting Illini hugged me, nearly crushing my ribs, before telling me that I'd better be taking care of Jess. I knew these men were just being protective of Jess, their eldest niece (or female cousin), but I felt like I was starting off in a deep hole.

Jess's grandmother, on the other hand, was giddy over meeting me. Within an hour after my arrival, she offered to lend me her engagement ring. Jess had been afraid that her grandmother would say something ignorant, like asking me if I ate dogs. I would have cracked up if she had asked that. I would have answered, "Dogs? No. It's best to get 'em when they're still puppies."

Jess would have *killed* me.

Now, to put this in context, I should tell you that whenever I talk to Jess about Chinese culture, I lie. She once asked me, "How come you never wear your shoes in the apartment?" and I told her, "It's a Chinese thing."

Another time, she said to me, "Honey, you are crazy for your pork chops, aren't you?" It's true. I love my pork chops and all things pork—pork loins, breakfast sausage, bacon, pulled pork, barbecued pork ribs, bacon-wrapped pork chops, bacon-wrapped bacon!—and I told her, "It's a Chinese thing."

When I was home alone one day, watching some girl-on-girl action on the Internet, she came home early and almost caught me. I had to slam shut my laptop. She asked if I was watching porn, and I told her, "For God's sake, woman, it's a Chinese thing!"

Jess used to think our racial joking was funny, but it got less funny when she met *my* parents, and suddenly being able to distinguish my bullshit from the real thing was the difference between her getting along with my folks and totally insulting them by accident. Jess had been *on* me with questions: "What's the difference between Chinese and Taiwanese?" "How does *feng shui* work?" "Chinese people don't really eat dogs, do they?"

It drives me crazy because, for all my talk about "It's a Chinese thing," I don't know crap. Just because my skin is Chinese, doesn't mean I know all about it. Yes, I was born and raised in a Chinese family, but I grew up in a suburb near Columbus, Ohio, a place not exactly known for its bustling Chinatown or its melting pot of ethnicities. Until I was an adult, I didn't have any Chinese friends. I had a few black friends and some Jewish friends, and a good friend from India, but I didn't have any more cross-cultural experiences than your average white person. For most of my life, I went around trying to pass for white—and succeeding, because even though I'm Chinese, I sound totally white. Even with my Chinese name, I went by Chip when I bussed tables at Damon's as a teenager, and I've gone by my initials CP for so long that I don't even answer to my Chinese name anymore. As long as we're all being polite, I can pass for white, or so I think, but when I walk into a dive bar in Indiana, I feel like I can hear all the locals muttering, "Nah, fella, you ain't white."

A few years ago, I started shooting pool at a bar in Lincoln Park, one of those places where you put your name on a chalkboard to get next on a pool table and, if you win, you keep the table until you get knocked off. These three other Chinese guys were always there, and this is one of those Lincoln Park bars where the only people of color there worked in the back. So one day I walked over to these three other guys, looked at them, looked at all the other white people, and said, "Dudes, we gotta be over quota here. One of us Chinamen is gonna have to leave."

We all cracked up, and after that we became friends. We started going to bars and restaurants together, and heading down to Chinatown for Chinese food, and it blew my mind that I could actually go to Chinatown with other people without feeling like I was a tour guide on a field trip, showing the tourists all the exotic sights.

Hanging out with these guys *defined* being Chinese to me. My grandfather would roll over in his grave to hear me say, "Screw the five thousand years of history, being Chinese means I've got friends that I can call chinks." But yeah, it meant that I had a group of friends that I belonged to. For all the things we learn from different people, it's also really comfortable to hang out with people who are like you, other artists and writers, or other gay men, or other people from the South, other folks in the service industry, other people like *you*. Not because you dislike people who are different, but you don't have to explain as much or be on your guard. You're comfortable in your own skin—literally. These guys I met shared the same problems and laughed at the same jokes. They were my tribe.

But for all that Jess wants to know about Chinese culture, real Chinese culture, I tell her, "I got nothing." And it drives her crazy because she worries that she'll never really belong to my family.

The Christmas dinner menu in Danville included turkey, greens with pork, mac and cheese (with bacon bits in it), and *ten* pounds of chitlins. Chitlins are pig intestines, if you didn't know. I told Jess's grandmother that the Chinese have a similar dish, but I never had real chitlins. When they're cooking, they smell pungent, but they taste good. Jess says they smell like ass. She doesn't eat chitlins. She doesn't eat pork, or beef, or turkey, or any meat at all.

Yes, at this feast of meat that her family was preparing, Jess was the one vegetarian in the whole extended family. On our way to dinner, we had to stop by Whole Foods to pick up a tofurkey meal just so she'd have something to eat. (Tofurkey, if you didn't know, is turkey, except made from tofu. It's not bad . . . it just needs more bacon on it.) Though her parents know that Jess is a vegetarian, they haven't gotten used to the idea of their daughter, whom they raised on R & B music and barbeque, growing up to be a vegetarian who practices yoga and prefers the Dave Matthews Band over Kanye West.

As the meal was just about ready—it was going to be buffet-style on the kitchen counter—Jess and her mother were in the kitchen. Jess's mom wore her hair in tight braids for the occasion and had on a Christmas sweater set. Jess wanted to make sure her tofurkey wouldn't disappear, so she whispered to her mom, "Don't draw any attention to my food . . . but could you make sure that no one eats any of it?"

Jess's mom responded by bellowing out to everyone, "Okay, don't anybody touch any of Jess's weirdo food!" Jess stomped out of the kitchen, and when I caught up to her, she growled at me, "It's always like this!" She glared through the wall towards her mom and muttered, "Just deal with it already!"

Then it turned out that her grandmother's house didn't have quite enough chairs for everyone, and after Jess's dad asked us gently if we could wait a while, we stood around in the kitchen, watching the uncles and aunts and cousins and her grandmother and her parents have Christmas dinner, until some of her cousins finished their meals and let us have their chairs. The two of us had dinner by ourselves at a small kitchen table, without the rest of the family.

After dinner, I was in the living room with Jess and a few of the uncles and cousins. Uncle Derek was quizzing Cousin Brian about living on the South Side of Chicago. Brian said, "Come on up for a visit. When you get downstairs from me, call, and I'll come get you."

Derek asked, "Call you? Why? Do I need to be scared?" Brian shrugged, and Derek leaned in for the joke: "What, are there black people where you live?" He pretended to be on the phone, his voice low and husky and frightened: "Brian, come get me. I see black people on the street!" Everyone in the room cracked up.

Everyone but me.

Could I laugh without seeming racist? Could I *not* laugh without seeming racist? I smiled with closed lips, not even sure myself whether I was forcing it or not. I was seated on the arm of the couch where Jess sat, and so it was easy for me to slip off to the kitchen to see if anyone needed help cleaning up. It was like another reminder: "No, motherfucker, you ain't black either." I can't fake Chinese, can't pass as white, and can't find a home in black, either. What the hell was I supposed to do?

Jess and I left for home the next day. The highway was still slushy from the snowstorm that had hit just before the holiday, and we saw dozens of cars and trucks that had been abandoned by the side of the road.

In the car, when Jess asked me, just to make conversation, what Chinese weddings were like, I lost my shit. I couldn't keep on lying or joking around or making up stories. "I DON'T KNOW!" I shouted at her. "I don't know about Chinese weddings, I don't know about shit!"

Jess was driving, and her voice was low as she asked, "What'd I say?"

I sighed and stared out the window. "I dunno. Sometimes I think that maybe your next boyfriend will be the right one. That he'll be black and Christian and successful, a man who knows at least where he came from."

She bit her lip hard and refused to look at me. "I don't want a next boyfriend."

We were on I-57, halfway between Champaign-Urbana and Chicago. It's like any interstate where you see McDonald's and Burger King and Wendy's: the lowest common denominator for what it means to be an American. For all we do to try to bridge the gap between races and cultures, ultimately, maybe the only thing everyone has in common is french fries.

We drove in silence. I thought about how the people who do Internet dating had the right idea: put all your baggage online and let the computers sort it out. Why date someone you meet in the bar, and maybe fall in love, only to find out that you can't get over your differences?

When Jess and I got back to Chicago, we unpacked our things and collapsed into bed. Our bedroom walls are covered with artwork, paintings and sketches that either our friends or we made. It's a tribute to what we hope to be, as artists or as friends of artists. It seemed like such a pipe dream as I lay there. I stared at the ceiling in the dark; I could tell by her breathing she hadn't fallen asleep. I broke the silence. "I know you don't wish I were black, but I just feel like an outsider with your family."

She turned, shifting so that her outside leg wrapped over my thighs and she hugged me. Her face nestled into my neck as she murmured, "If you're on the outside, then that's where I want to be, too. Hell, I'm the black sheep in my own family."

She rolled over onto her back and sighed. I knew she was thinking about her mother.

In the dark of our bedroom, I asked her, "What does a black sheep sound like?"

She thought about it for a second, and then she said, "Baaaa . . . nigga!"

We laughed, and afterwards she said, "Maybe we can make our own tribe."

"Yeah, I'd like that."

With that, we fell asleep, holding hands throughout the night.

HERE, CAPTURE SOMETHING

BY ANDREW REILLY

SpiceJet Airlines flight 0S 295, two hours nonstop on a near-empty 737 from Delhi to Mumbai: I spent most of our time in the air looking out the window; the lack of announcement from the cockpit suggested the pilot had opted for a nap; quietly proving herself smarter than either of us, and the beautiful girl back in seat 23D with the dark hair and the light brown skin instead spent the whole trip hiding behind a copy of *National Geographic*.

A smoother, more confident version of me might have asked her what she was reading, or subtly mentioned the thousands upon thousands of miles I had put between myself and my terrible apartment in the Wicker Park neighborhood of Chicago, or made a casual reference to how I, at the wise old age of twenty-six, was about to abandon a promising career in software engineering for a more theoretically glamorous life of writing, not unlike a young Ernest Hemingway, but trading the cafés of post-war Paris for the seedier bars and half-developed cities of India.

I, however, was not smooth, nor was I confident, nor did I have any real idea how to talk to intriguing women aboard domestic flights in foreign countries, reducing our interaction to an awkward wave of my right hand after we landed as though to say, "You can go first," but hoping she would interpret that as, "You have very pretty green eyes." She smiled, stepped past me and off of the plane, and disappeared into the shuffle of Shivaji International Airport, a beautiful ghost passing through on her way to someplace else.

But when I saw her later that afternoon in the Mumbai marketplace, she was *someone*: she was the girl from flight OS 295, which meant I was also the guy from flight OS 295, which meant I had context, which meant I had some stupid excuse for talking to this girl, which was all to say I was *in*.

"I need your help," I said, trying not to move as a spoke, lest I drown in sweat in the brutal Indian heat. "I don't know what to buy for my sister back home."

"Oh, is that so?" she teased, her voice carrying just a hint of a British accent. "You couldn't ask me about that on the plane?"

"Wait, you were on my flight?" (I can admit now my feigned shock was less than convincing.)

"This might be a surprise," she said, almost laughing at me now. "But buzz cut white people tend to stick out in this country." Touché.

"My name's Jaya," she continued. "From my Indian grandmother." The crowd bustled behind us, barefoot old women selling fresh fruit and young men hawking some extremely convincing designer knockoffs. "And from my British father, a useful tightness with money," she joked. "So come on, I'll teach how to shop in this place." She took my hand—her fingers wrapped lightly around mine, just enough to guide but not enough to hold—as we walked through the marketplace in search of bargains on throw pillows and jewelry. Between buying bracelets and haggling for shirts I only guessed my sister would wear, I asked her about the camera she was carrying. "I work freelance," she explained. "Magazines, postcards, whatever comes up. For you, this might be vacation but for me, this week is also an assignment."

I told her about my big plan to become a writer. "Then I'm

going to show you how to take pictures. You won't get any good jobs if all you can do is scribble some words. Here," she said, handing me the camera. "Capture something beautiful."

I leaned back, pointing the lens towards her. Click. "Cute," she said. "But you didn't let it focus. Look at this picture, my hair's blowing all over the place!" She took hold of the camera, turning some dials and pressing some buttons before handing it back to me. "Don't think about what's in the shot," she said. "Just think about what you see. Come on, I'll show you."

We walked together through the city, taking turns shooting the opulent wealth and abhorrent squalor sitting side-by-side. Centuries of blatant class warfare had formed two cities at once, but rather than separate them by roads or rivers, the people of Mumbai had simply built on top of each other, miles upon miles of slums collapsing at the doorsteps of billionaires' estates.

"Take a picture of that," she said, pointing to one miniature palace in particular. Trying my best to impress her, I turned the lens to catch the sun's rays bursting over the top of the marble and wrought-iron fence protecting it from would-be invaders. Click.

"Not bad," she said before fiddling with the knobs, stepping backwards and ducking down on one knee before shooting. "But there's more over there than just the house." She turned the LCD screen so I could see it: the house, yes, but in hers that marble and wrought-iron fence I had focused upon ran towards the lower-left corner of the frame and trailed off into the horizon, the estate rising up like some luxurious volcano in this sea of filth, garbage lining the dirt sidewalks as a man lay in the street, his right leg missing and skin badly flaking.

"The man who lives there is a friend of our family from my father's days working for the British ambassador to India," she explained. "We came here to Mumbai often when I was a child, which my mother loved because she could see her family, even though some of her relatives never forgave her for marrying a *gora*."

"What's a *gora*?" I asked.

She paused before saying, "It's a Hindi word." Then, pointing at my arm: "White man."

"What would they think of you being out on the town with a *gora?*" I asked.

"My older relatives would be upset, and my younger relatives wouldn't care," she said. "But I don't tell my family everything." I thought about everyone I knew back home, about who would be happy I had met this intelligent, headstrong woman and who would be angry she had brown skin; perhaps she and I had more in common than I realized.

Moments became hours and hours became days, and *my* vacation quietly became *our* vacation, she acting as tour guide, cultural ambassador, and co-conspirator all at once. Each day, we would dine in a different café, giving a new story to the revolving cast of waiters: we're here on business; we're on our honeymoon; we're shooting a Bollywood remake of *Star Wars* where I play Han Solo and she plays Princess Leia.

One afternoon we walked along the water to the Gateway of India, the archway facing out onto the city's eastern harbor. She pointed out a group of three young Indian men loitering along the fence around the monument, all scowling in my direction, and immediately I recognized that look: when I was twenty-three, I'd gone on two dates with a black woman—not a long relationship by any means, but still long enough for her friends to stare me down in eerily similar fashion the first and only time I met them.

"They don't like us," Jaya said.

"No." I sighed. "They just don't like me. *Gora.* They think I've stolen something from them." *Stupid!* I scolded myself. *What's the matter with you? Who calls a woman "something?"*

"But look over there," I joked, pointing towards a thirty-ish looking white man standing by himself, his Christos polo shirt and Queensland Rugby baseball cap giving him away as an Australian. "That guy loves me." Taking my gesturing as some kind of invitation, the Australian walked over to us, tipping his hat to her before stopping in front of me.

"I just want to tell you," he said, his gaze alternating between my eyes and her chest, "It's nice to know I'm not the only one here who's into the brownies."

The Australian went on his way; I turned to Jaya, trying to apologize, but she was having none of that. "I've learned not to listen," she said, waving it off. "This country doesn't treat its women too well, even while it dresses us in the finest pashmina and drapes us in beautiful jewelry. I think it rubs off on the men who come to visit."

What men? I wondered. *What visits? Was I one of those men? No, come on. But she's really pretty, so does that make me—wait, this silence is getting awkward; do something, Andrew.*

"Well," I finally said, "If it makes you feel better, I don't have a fetish for Indian girls. But I'm not gonna lie: the British thing is *hot.*"

Jaya giggled, leaned in, and kissed me with almost furious purpose; those three young Indian men finally walked off in disgust.

On the last day of her assignment, we stood along the western edge of the city, watching the boats sailing out of the harbor towards the Arabian Sea. We had talked a lot on those Mumbai streets, about travel and life goals and families and friends—those things that, with time, build the bridge from first-date small talk to latter-stage big talk. But the more we talked about all of those things, about the Premier League and the World Series the White Sox had just won and whether or not New Order was a better band than Joy Division and, yes, about my terrible apartment in Wicker Park, the more I noticed what we didn't talk about: home, as in, what happened when we each returned to each of ours. Our time was running out, but the longer we avoided the issue, the more I understood why we danced around it: neither of us knew the answer.

"Here," she said, smiling brightly as she handed me the camera. "Show me how much I've taught you."

I put my eye to the viewfinder and aimed out into the sea, following a pair of sailboats out of the harbor and thinking about this delicate moment we were stumbling towards, she and I with the whole world before us, forced to decide whether to drop anchor or whether to sail where the winds took us. Click.

I handed the camera back to her and steeled myself. "What happens after tonight? I mean, when you leave, what do we do?"

She lowered her head for a moment and, taking a deep breath, said "I like you very much, Andrew," her voice quivering as she spoke. "I know we just met, but I like . . . us."

She rested her hands in mine as the late afternoon sun beat down on us, finally raising her eyes to meet mine. "So come back to England with me."

What? "What?"

"Come back to England with me," she said. "You told me you're bored with Chicago and ready for a new life. Come with me. Be with me."

And for a moment, I could do it—I could imagine it: she and I, the hottest item on London's social map, my words flourishing under the tender care of my new muse and her photography opening my eyes to fantastic worlds I couldn't even dream of. Jaya and I around town, a sea of onlookers parting before us, flashbulbs burning ahead of miles upon miles of words written about us; all the important gallery openings, all the most exclusive clubs, the finest of high-end restaurants and the best of the low-rent pubs, there we'd be, the art world's newest power couple, rising literary star Andrew Reilly and world-famous photographer Jaya . . . Jaya . . . what was her last name, anyway?

And come to think of it, what else didn't I know about this woman?

And what, really, did she know about me? Did I really want to move to England to live with a girl I had just met last week on vacation? Who did we think we were?

I wanted to say something beautiful, something poetic and

wondrous that wouldn't let her down, something that didn't sound like an excuse, something that would show her how badly I wanted to hold on to her but all that came out was: "I can't."

Jaya smiled and put her hand on my cheek as those pretty green eyes began to well up. "I understand," she said. "You have to go. We both do." And what killed me was not the sun slowly fading into the water, or the boats setting sail to shores unknown, or the knowledge that I was witnessing an ending in slow motion; what killed me was the simple way she stressed "both" slightly, just enough to guide, but not enough to hold.

We pulled each other close, her lips pressing softly to mine for what must have been hours, days, forever, until I stepped back, understanding this was only going to become more difficult the longer we held on. I turned away from her slowly, finally forging my way back into the crowded street to start the long walk to my hotel, stopping briefly to look back towards where I had left her, thinking maybe I could form some final, perfect memory before she vanished forever, but by then she had ducked behind her camera, already back to work. I waved goodbye to nothing in particular and walked on.

I returned home later that month into the gaping maw of another awful Chicago winter, right back to my terrible apartment in Wicker Park, but vowing to stick to the plan as best I could: quit my job, go to graduate school, start building that portfolio, become that glamorous writer. It should go without saying that some parts came easier than others.

Still, more often than I wanted to admit, I would catch myself thinking of that afternoon by the harbor, wondering if I had been a coward for letting her go. Other times, something would trigger the thought for me: a girl passing by on the street with even the faintest resemblance; a tourist and his camera trying to take home a small piece of Chicago; something in the news briefly mentioning England.

I should have gone with her, I would tell myself.

Then: *No, I shouldn't have.*

Then: *Yes, I should have.*

Then: *Forget it, she's gone.*

Then: *And whose fault is that?*

They were ideas I would keep coming back to, ideas which I just assumed had no real resolution and never would, until one afternoon that spring, when I returned home to find a heavily padded package in the mailbox with no return address but bearing numerous international postmarks, inside of which I found a CD and a short, handwritten letter:

Dear Andrew,

I thought you might like having these. I know I do.

Best wishes,

Jaya

Sitting down at my desk and placing the disc into my computer, I watched the images fill my screen, alternately gorgeous and terrible, the subjects vaguely familiar, and after a moment I suddenly realized what I was looking at: Jaya that first afternoon in the marketplace, her long black hair dancing in the dusty Indian breeze; the old man selling silver bracelets in the plaza; the boats heading into the sunset; all the pictures we had taken. Together.

But after all the scenery and stills came six black and white shots I'd never seen, but which so perfectly explained everything about us, and our brief time together, better than any scribbled words of mine ever could.

In the first three, a lone male walks down a busy street, away from the photographer and increasingly obscured by the commotion around him. He moves further into the crowd, pale skin and buzz cut the only things setting him apart from the ocean of people surrounding him. In the fourth, the camera zooms in as he looks over his shoulder and waves to an unseen person out of frame; in the fifth, the subject lowers his head and wipes his eyes; in the sixth and final frame, the young man disappears completely, and the crowd bustles on without him.

I leaned back in my chair, took a deep breath, and let myself feel the weight of the image before me. Here, now, all these days and weeks and months after she and I had parted, alone in a room she would never know, the two of us half a world apart, staring into this picture that so neatly contained nothing yet somehow captured everything, I finally—*finally*—understood what she had been trying to show me all along: even if I wasn't there, she could *see* me.

And I knew that I, if I looked closely enough, could see her, too. ▥

COVERGIRL
BY KIMBERLEE SOO

I am eleven years old, sitting in my sister's car. It is my Special Day. She is applying lipstick at a red light with the expertise of someone who now goes to college. The light turns green, and she sticks the lipstick tube between her front teeth and reaches to change gears. Trina drives a stick shift. She is strong. I'm going to drive a stick shift.

"Here," she says, and hands me the tube. My heart does a tap dance. "It's more orange-red," she says without looking at me. "You'd be better in blue-red."

Trina drives with the window down and doesn't care if her naturally blonde hair whips her in the face because she knows she is beautiful. I take the tube from Trina's hand and remove the lid. My hands are trembling as I slide the slippery smoothness across my lips. I delicately replace the lid, my lips doing some strange spasm, and Trina says, "Just throw it in my purse," and I do, slowly, so I can get a good look inside. I see her powder case, and I study the colors of her eye shadow, imagining them on my almond-shaped eyes. I ask her what the plastic pink compact is and she says, "None of your business," and grabs her purse from my hand and tosses it in the back seat. As usual, I've pushed my luck.

At the next stoplight the shiny Chevy truck in the lane to our left revs its engine. The front seat is packed with high school boys. I know this because they have the same Hilhi Spartans decal on their window that my older brother has on his clarinet case. They glance our way—Trina's way—and call out, "Hey you!" and I waffle between shrinking and desperately wanting to be seen 'cause I'm wearing lipstick! Trina laughs, her mouth wide open. And with a head tossed back, braces finally off, killer laugh says, "Hey what?" And I think, *Brilliant! She always knows just what to say!*

A boy, with his shirtsleeve rolled up high enough to reveal part of a tattoo, leans out the window, his hand resting on the mirror. A hand that looks wide enough to cover the entire surface of my face. I imagine this briefly and think of my lips leaving a fresh mark on the palm of that boy's hand, and my cheeks turn red. But I know he isn't looking at me. It's gonna take a lot more than orange-red lipstick.

The light has turned green, and I am ready to have my sister back, but she has shifted slightly in their direction, both perfect breasts pointing their way. The radio is playing Joan Jett and the Blackhearts, and I try desperately to move coolly, inhibited by the seatbelt Trina insists I wear. Her shoulder strap fits ideally between her perfect breasts and makes her T-shirt even tighter. My T-shirt is long and baggy and covers my butt when I stand, and I have pulled my shoulder strap down under my right arm so it won't rub against my neck (or accentuate the flatlands of my chest). The tattooed boy begs, "Come ooooon, what's your naaaaame?" for the hundredth time. Trina just laughs. He leans out farther, and I imagine him sliding all the way into our car. In this moment, with that truckload of boys peeping in, I would give anything to have Trina's breasts. I sit, trying to be relaxed and tall with my black bangs cutting straight across my forehead, the sweat beginning to form at the hairline. I wish we were moving.

Trina's car smells of cigarettes and Angelfire, recently sprayed. She tries to hide her smoking habit from me, because she knows somewhere deep that I will do whatever she does (and because she isn't convinced that she is a smoker).

The boys are still trying to get Trina's number, and I want to scream, *"Hello, this is my special day! I get to do what I want, and I don't have to do chores, and no one can talk in code or tell me to scram!"* but I don't. Instead I fumble through the cassette tapes shoved in the glove compartment and then I study the floor mats. There are empty Tab cans, sugar free gum wrappers and a copy of *Shape* magazine. Trina is healthy. She works out at a gym where the women walk around the locker room naked and the bulky shiny men wear yellow spandex.

Finally. We drive.

"I think the guy in the middle was checkin' you out," she says. I start giggling manically. "No way!"

"Totally," she says. "With that lipstick, you look at least thirteen."

While I want to believe her, I can tell she is trying to be nice because she starts biting her lip like she does when she's nervous or lying or has to sing a solo at church.

We park at the mall, and I take crazy long Trina-sized steps to keep up. It makes my calves hurt. But I can't slow down; can't let her see that I am struggling. Trina is *cool*. And when I am with her, when I can keep up with her, I am *cool*.

I haven't been to the mall since my mom took me bra shopping earlier in the school year and insisted on coming into the fitting room with me. Trina asks me if I want an Orange Julius, and I say, "Nah, I'm not hungry," when I'm actually starving, but I don't want to mess up my lipstick.

We run into Fred Myers (which is the kind of place where I can spend a whole summer's allowance. It's like K-Mart meets Payless Shoe Source meets the Dollar Store). Trina needs nylons. I go with, but veer into the make-up aisle scanning the rows until I see it. CoverGirl. *Yeah*. I am sweating and eager and breathless, but cannot find a lipstick called Blue Red. But, I do find the eye shadow that Trina wears, and I feel such a rush of victory, I actually consider slipping it into my pocket and walking. But I don't.

Instead, I skitter through the aisles trying to find my sister, who turns out to be already in the checkout line. I hold my breath and get in line behind her, wondering if she will stop me from making this dangerously adult purchase. The cashier rings me up, and I pull out my sparkly pink plastic wallet with the little mirror in the flap and fake rhinestone closure and think, *Someday I'll have a red leather purse and matching high heels and credit cards and no bangs.* I make eye contact with Trina, and she smiles for a half a second, and then she is distracted by Luke and Laura on the cover of *Soap Opera Digest*.

My hand is sticky as I hold the bag, and I tell Trina I have to go to the bathroom. "Meet me in the food court. I need caffeine," she says, and we head off in opposite directions.

I am so close.

Once situated in a stall on the far end away from the door I wipe my hands on my jeans near the spot I have been trying to work into a hole. I get my wallet/mirror and then pull out my first ever CoverGirl eye shadow. I peel off the back, careful not to damage the instructions. There is a diagram, and I can see that I am just three easy steps away from changing my life forever.

Step one tells me to apply the lightest shade to my entire eyelid. I do this while trying to keep the soft sparkly blue from dusting my black eye brows. Niiiiiiiice.

Step two. I take the skinny side of the application wand and the darkest shade and drag it across my lash line. I do one eye and then the next. And then I go back and forth and back and forth trying to make them look the same!

I read step three: apply contour shade to the eyelid crease. I grip the application wand and steady my gaze in the mirror. I bring the wand to my eye. And then I freeze.

Only now do I see it.

I have no crease.

No crease in my eyelid for the contour shade. No place for blending. No place to create depth.

There is no step three for me.

I will never be beautiful.

Ever. *Never ever.*

The stall feels crowded, the walls are pressing in and I am dizzy. I slide off the toilet seat onto the cool tiles and lift the lid, resting my chin on the porcelain edge. My head could fit in that toilet bowl, I think. I could plunge my head into that filthy water . . . but then I envision Trina, having finished her diet soda (and maybe small fries if she plans on going to the gym tonight) looking for me, making her way toward the ladies room, finding me, face down—

I wipe off steps one and two and hurry to the food court. I can't tell if Trina is checking me for signs of her eye shadow because I am careful not to look at her.

We start walking back toward the exit and Trina catches her breath and says, "Wow, check him out, he's from the gym." She exhales, and I see the red rise in her cheeks, and she starts biting her lip.

Then everything goes slo-mo, and I can't feel my feet.

Coming toward us is this amazing boy, no, this amazing *man*, with faded jeans slightly frayed at the edges, Doc Martens squeaking as he approaches. He has gorgeous guitar player hands, and I nearly gasp when he reaches up and pushes his thick chocolaty hair (à la Rick Springfield) away from his mile-long lashes. This guy is magic. Trina's hips sway with each step. The guy slides his guitar player hands deep into his pockets. Trina flips her naturally blonde hair over her shoulder with an ease I know she does not feel.

And then, when the guy is inches away from Trina, I see him lift his chin slightly and smile a flawless "never even needed braces" smile up at Trina. He is now at a complete stop, body turning in towards her, an opening line poised on his recently licked lips.

But Trina doesn't slow down, doesn't smile. I slam back to reality as we speed away from the magical guy. A few seconds later Trina says, "Too bad."

I'm so confused. What did she see? What flaw did I miss?

We are almost to the car when she says again, "Too bad."

I stay completely silent hoping she will forget I am there and just keep talking.

"You're lucky you're short."

I don't answer because I am sure that she is making fun of me.

"You'll be able to date anyone you want," she says. "It totally sucks to be this tall."

I am surprised. And *delighted*. I steal a glance at her. My beautiful sister. Then I notice for the first time ever how she slumps her shoulders when she walks, like she's apologizing for being way up there.

And I think of the family picture we recently took. Trina is center, the edge of the shot just skimming the top of her head. I am in front of her, little and cut off at the knees. Neither of us fits. I imagine someone pulling the camera back just slightly to accommodate both of us, so you can see all of Trina and all of me.

Trina knows I'm watching her. She looks over at me and winks.

"Yeah, they're gonna love you."

Maybe, I think. And then we walk. And I take me-sized steps all the way back to the car. ▥

FOREIGNER IN A STRAIGHT LAND
BY J. ADAMS OAKS

Men.

Men were terrible, awful, scary, sweaty, cocky, dangerous creatures. I mean, I know. I'm one of them. I get that finally. But before I came out of the closet, I felt like there were two types of people: human beings and Men with a capital *M*. I was just a human being—all lower case letters. They were so alien to me: throwing footballs and slapping each other on the back, skateboarding and not talking much, and when they did say something, they spoke in a code I had no translation for. It was like I was a foreigner in a straight land, so for a long time I hid as best I could. Don't get me wrong: I still moved amongst the natives. I learned their ceremonies and ate the local food. I even imitated their language and dated their women when necessary. So it's ironic that it took moving to a foreign country for me to find my native land and really start living life, instead of watching it all go by.

I came out in Spain. It wasn't until a year later when I got back to the States that I found out that coming out was all the rage and there was even somebody named RuPaul singing about it.

161

Everybody was bi-curious and gay-friendly and trying real real hard to find something gay inside of them. And I remember spending many late nights reassuring straight friends that they didn't have a closet to come out of. Like my friend Beth, who told me she thought she'd fallen in love with her female Spanish professor.

"Like, I mean, how do I know?" she asked me. "I can't stop thinking about her, and I can't wait to get to her class, and sometimes I think about kissing her, maybe."

"Well, you could be gay," I told her. "But, Beth, you know what lesbians do, right?"

"Not really," she said. And when I told her the down-and-dirty—I mean, the *down-and-dirty*—her face wrinkled up, and she said, "Eeeew."

"Then you are *not* gay, Beth, 'cause that's what lesbians do. They actually *love* it, gross as it may sound."

Anyway, for me—before that fashion hit the streets—I'd spent most of my twenty years trying damned hard to stay in the closet. I had never met one openly gay person. I'd only heard of "The Gays" or "Homosexuals," but all those men were lurking in bathrooms, or dressing like women for some reason, or were priests and gym teachers touching little boys. I wasn't any of that. I was just a guy who happened to really like other guys. I mean *really* like guys. Those poor girls I'd had to date, well . . . let's just say I was good at pretending I'd passed out, and as a virgin, I spent every single day pretending I wasn't looking at every single man that passed by. So when I finally got to Spain, I was pretty much screwed. Here were these olive-skinned, dark-wavy-haired passionate Marlboro Men—capital *M*—strutting around making my head woozy. But there still was a wall up between me and other guys: I had no flirting skills, no dating skills, and no idea how other guys met each other. It made me feel even more foreign, and it made Spain feel even more surreal. It wasn't home, you know? My folks weren't there. My best friends were far away. Everyone was a stranger. For God's sake, I was speaking a different language so much my brain hurt.

I gotta tell you I did fall in love there—with Madrid. The city is more Chicago than New York or Paris; it's a lot working-class and a little too serious. And it's not all gypsies, bullfights, and sangria (though there's a lot of that). It's also all-night bars and lazy afternoons at a café in el Parque del Retiro with friends and moped rides through honking traffic jams surrounded by romantic old architecture. I'd almost say Madrid was my first true love, but that wouldn't be fair to Joe. See, Joe was this guy I met on my abroad program.

It's February 13, 1991. There is no such thing as the Internet or cell phones or laptop computers. And the song I rewind on my Walkman again and again is "Freedom" by George Michael.

I'm at a surprise party for Joe, and he gets a birthday card with a shirtless guy on it. *Hmmm . . .* I think. *Interesting.* The girls giggle, assuming everybody knows Joe's out of the closet, and my heart races. I try not to stare, but study him in detail: he's cute, quiet, kind of sulky, and pretty much a regular everyday guy. Is that possible?

I wish him a happy birthday, shake his hand and leave, because at this point I can't really deal with him since I'm living in a really deep, dark, melodramatic hole of loneliness where nobody else could actually understand what I was going through. Actually, I was living in a neighborhood called Alfonso XIII with two guys just behind a highway billboard in a little brick house that we called "The Shit Shack." It had no phone and a wood-burning stove we fed with old telephone poles. It had a refrigerator in the living room and a gas tank for cooking and hot water. Those tanks were called *bombónes* because of their shape, like orange-wrapped chocolates. Almost a week after Joe's birthday party, I used that tank in the bathroom to try to kill myself. It finally all made complete sense: the best option really was death. It would make things easier on my family, on my friends. There'd be no shame. No having to wait for me to die of the AIDS I'd surely get. I stuffed newspaper in the cracks around the door and window, separated the line from the tank, sat in the bathtub, and cried.

But that shitty fucking house just had too many holes in it, and wind whipped through cracks around the window. Man, that pissed me off. But it got my sobbing to slow down. I reattached the gas line, removed the newspaper and thought, *I guess I can try talking to that Joe guy. He seems pretty normal. For a Man . . .*

So that night, I walked four blocks to the closest pay phone and called Joe. I practiced a casual tone before I dialed. "Hey, uh, man, you around tomorrow? Can I stop by? It's no big deal. I just wanted to hang out." I'd never spent time with him before one-on-one, but he didn't seem to mind, said to stop by the next day.

God, I remember February 21, 1991, so well: the colors, the sounds, the crisp sunny day as I chain-smoked Fortuna cigarettes all the way to Joe's place. He met me at the door to his apartment building just south of Atocha—that's the train station that would be bombed thirteen years later; where we stood, we would have felt the explosion. Joe wore his red Gore-Tex jacket with the hood, because there was still a nip in the air. He brought his camera, because he's a fantastic photographer.

"Hi," he said.

"Hi," I said.

"Thought I'd take some pictures. Wanna walk around the neighborhood?"

I could only nod, because I thought I was going to die. What was I thinking? I couldn't do this . . . Jesus, shame is such a heavy coat to wear, isn't it?

The short walk down Paseo de las Delicias felt like miles. Small talk had never been so painful, and words had never been a struggle for me, but the three I wanted to say made me feel like I was going to puke. I needed to sit down and rest my brain, so we found a little park tucked between some high-rise apartments. Joe and I sat on either end of the same bench. It was hot in the sun. Kids played while mothers watched, waving fans to cool their faces. "Um . . . ," I said and looked down. "I gotta tell you something." Between my feet, in the red dirt, cockroaches ate bread left for pigeons. Joe snapped photos.

Don't puke, I told myself. *Don't puke.* He took a couple shots of me. I didn't even know this guy, but he was about to become the most important person in my life whether he wanted to or not. Just by smiling. Just by listening. Just by understanding. "Joe, I gotta tell you . . . "

And I said it.

And nothing changed.

God, it sounds so dramatic, but the only surprising thing was how normal the world still felt. Kids still played. Cockroaches still skittered. Joe still smiled. I took the deepest breath I'd ever taken, and then we talked. Or, rather, I asked questions, and he answered them as best he could. The poor guy was hardly out himself, but he still did have "experience." I remember asking things like: "So how do gay people know each other are gay?" "Have you ever been to the gay neighborhood?" "In a couple, is one guy the man and the other guy the woman?" And, "What's that rainbow flag for?" On and on for—well, not just for that night, but days and days. "Hey, I don't have to like leather, do I?"

See, the trick with coming out is that it's not just that one step: "I'm gay!" and everything is hunky-dory. I'd only just started a process that happens for the rest of my life, a process of learning to tell the truth and getting rid of that damned shame. So there I was in Madrid, practicing being honest, the knots in my stomach loosening a bit each time I said, "I need to tell you something: I'm gay." And then waited for a response. These are some of the reactions I got, in no particular order:

"I'm so happy you finally figured it out! Congratulations!"

"*Vale, vale. Coño. ¿Y qué más da?*"

"Boy, that explains a lot. You've been acting so weird lately."

And then there was Tom, my roommate at "The Shit Shack." I was so afraid he was going to punch me in the face that I took him all the way to the fancy McDonald's on la Gran Vía, because I figured he wouldn't make a scene in public. Instead, he said, "So? What do you want? A cookie? A trophy?" I got to thinking: you know,

165

Tom was right. What did I want? It wasn't like a badge of courage. I didn't do anything special. Being gay was just one little tiny piece of me, right? Like my hair color or my shoe size, really. Why was I making such a big deal out of it?

But that's not what you want to hear about, do you? You want to hear about the sex. Well, yes, Joe and I would eventually start dating. We'd take a walk down el Paseo del Prado and into the Botanical Gardens and decide to be boyfriends, and *yes* finally I would shed the burden of virginity. I would tell him, "It's time to get rid of it. And you're going to help me." So during spring break on the southern coast of Spain, in a room with a bunk bed, while our unsuspecting friends snored in rooms around us, the night before we took a ferryboat to Africa, escorted by flying fish and dolphins, we did it. And it was good. More importantly, after twenty-one long years, *I* did it. And then it was gone.

But that's not the story I like to tell. Usually, I like to remember the moment I knew things would get better. A week or two after that day in the park, before I'd come out to anyone else and before we'd started dating, Joe and I went on a trip with our study-abroad group to Córdoba, an ancient Roman town in Andalusia. And after a full day of sightseeing, a late night of drinking, Joe and I snuck off to take a walk. We wondered outside the city wall, across a stone bridge, along the river, into a moonlit playground to sit on the swings. I started in on my usual grilling: "Have you told your parents yet?" "Do you know any Spanish gay guys?" "Do you think you *look* gay?" On and on, Joe patiently answering, gently teasing me while this little bit of tension began to form between us. The city had quieted down, and it was getting chilly, so we headed back to the hotel. Our shoulders bumped occasionally as we walked back. And I felt okay. I mean, I didn't feel so bad all the time anymore. I felt normal. And I hoped his shoulder would bump me again.

We had separate rooms, so Joe walked me to mine to say goodnight. Before he left, he leaned up and kissed me on the lips. Not hard or long, but enough. Then he looked me in the eyes and mumbled, "That's just how gay people say goodbye. They kiss on the lips. Um. Even just friends." And off he went. I just stood there, leaning against the wall. My first kiss. No, I mean, I'd smooched girls before, like the rebel girl in black behind my high school, and popular girls, sexy girls, smart girls, foreign girls, all with my eyes open, bored, and trying hard to like it.

This was the real thing. This was the feeling everybody else was talking about. Now I understood nectar and skin and electricity and blossoms and winks and nudges. That kiss explained romance novels and clichéd lines, mood-lighting and rose-colored lenses. All that in an instant. From just one kiss. Like a bee sting or a splinter or a sneeze, *that kiss* made me start to get life, made me want to really live it, and not be such a foreigner anymore.

HERE COMES TROUBLE

BY RANDALL ALBERS

"Here comes trouble." You remember walking into a roomful of adults as a kid, and you'd hear that? And now, you come in this bar tonight, spot a hot woman in a tight dress or a smokin' guy in tight jeans, and you're the one saying it, "Here comes trouble." You can just *see* what's coming, but does that mean you'll stay out of it? *Hell*, no. You buy the person a Makers, and then another, maybe a third, and the next thing you know, it's summer and you're into all the intensity and the complications and the long, long, *long* discussions about The Relationship—and wondering how the heck you got here. Turns out you bought more than Maker's. You bought yourself some deep-shit trouble.

Sometimes, trouble comes looking for you, but sometimes you have to go out looking for *it*, just to jolt yourself alive again. That's the kind I've gone after. Of course, things don't always turn out the way you planned.

I grew up on a Minnesota farm, surrounded by families with kids who took over the farm, then had kids of their own who took over the farm. All so predictable. I wanted *more*. Like lots of farm kids, I spent long, winter days lost in stories—*Old Yeller, To Kill a Mockingbird, The Winter of Our Discontent, The Agony and the Ecstasy*—abridged novels arriving each month in the Reader's Digest Condensed Books. Ah, the passion, the romance of those worlds! They fed my wanderlust, and the first chance I got, I escaped to New Orleans for college, later studied abroad, and, after graduating, went back to hitchhike around England, Spain, and Morocco. I was out to find myself.

Along the way, I met a woman. And how many stories of trouble start out like that? Nora was smart, athletic, blond, with green eyes and high cheekbones—and even more intense about living a different life than I was. We read *The Alexandria Quartet* riding trains in Europe, the Romantic poets hiking Wordworth's Lake District, Kazantzakis sailing a tramp steamer to Mykonos with black-wrapped women carrying crates of chickens. I was head over heels in love. Hot-blood love. Nerve-singing love. Mad, bad, dangerous-to-know love. But spiritual, too, of course!

Eventually, we got married and hunkered down against the hawk, that slicing winter wind, while I finished a degree at the University of Chicago, then started another. One night, sitting on the scuffed floor of our sparsely furnished garden apartment reading Keats to each other by candlelight, I suddenly had a vision of my life rolling out before me like some goddamn carpet: finish my coursework, write my dissertation, get a job at some pastoral place like Carleton or Knox, teach, write lit. crit., get tenure, and go on teaching until one day I pitched face-down on my books in the florescent silence of the library and died.

"I'm not sure I can do this anymore," I told her.

A look of hope came to her face. "It's not exactly the Zorba life, is it," she said, repeating our oft-quoted mantra, "A man needs a little madness, or else he never dares cut the rope and be free.'"

"I ain't free," I said, thinking of the soul-shattering competition and literary grandstanding in my U. of C. classes. "But I've never quit anything in my life."

"A man needs a little madness . . . ," she said again, smiling.

And like that, the decision that we'd been coming to for months was made. Instead of writing a book about Romantic dreams, I'd live them. I announced my intention to leave the grad program in a classic bridge-burning letter to the chair. The program was intolerable, I told him. I was valued only for what I could produce, not for who I was—I'm sure I said *whom* I was—and to call the English Department part of the humanities was a misnomer, since there was nothing humane about it.

I know. Not smart, right? Goddamn pretentious, in fact. But I told you, I wanted *more*. I was looking for trouble.

We loaded a U-Haul and headed west, feeling free, wild— glorying in Nebraska's dreamlike plains, Wyoming's open high country, Colorado's majestic Rockies, Utah's shimmering salt flats, Nevada's rugged deserts as we plunged mile after mile toward California, destination of dreams. I didn't care what lay ahead. I just needed madness.

We moved into a converted chicken coop in the rolling, sun-drenched hills outside of Petaluma, a ramshackle affair with a hump in the floor that sent any spilled drink sliding right off toward the walls. We dubbed it the Funky Farm. My California dream—here with my love, no responsibilities, no labels, ready to learn who the hell Randy Albers really was.

Turned out I was a guy who couldn't get a job. With Berkeley puking out lit PhDs, I managed only a part-time gig teaching at a naval base, another bucking hay for a farmer. Meanwhile, with Nora working at a halfway house three days a week, I spent long stretches alone, often lonely, studying organic gardening, self-hypnosis, Senoi lucid dreaming—and learning to field train Boz, my new Gordon Setter puppy.

After a year of finding myself—and finding mainly that I was pretty boring—Nora inherited some money, and we bought a house in the apple orchards outside of Sebastopol where everyone was hiding out from something—young hippies and criminals on the lam in homemade shacks selling feathered earrings and roach clips to tourists or pushing home-grown grass harvested from monster plants hidden deep in the woods. Ah, the Zorba life, I thought, living off the land, living free. I dove into working on the house—painting, doing carpentry, sanding floors—everything but electrical work, which I wouldn't touch.

That's how I met Charlie.

You think you've had troubles? Well, if there were a Taxonomy of Troubles, Charlie'd be a long way up the chart. Short, thin, with a cap always pulled low over his narrow forehead, he'd once worked a job cutting metal in a press. He'd stick a sheet between the jaws, hit a button, the press would close, a sharp knife would slice a precise chunk off, rise, he'd shove the next sheet in, hit the button again. I'd once run a similar press in a plastics factory. I'd drop a soap-bar-sized piece of plastic into each of eight cavities in the mold, then pull two long levers that would close the jaws; a half-minute later they'd part, and there'd be eight hot plastic plates. When I asked the foreman why I needed to pull both levers to close the press, he told me, "To keep your hands out of the way." Charlie's machine didn't have levers, and one day, he's shoving sheets of metal in, hitting the button, pulling sheets out again, moving and moving, and, sure enough, his rhythm got thrown off, he hit the button while his hand was still in the press, and it closed, chopping off the middle three fingers and pretty well chewing up the other two.

Instead of sitting around collecting disability for the rest of his days, he decided to become an electrician. And what a worker he was! He'd trained his left hand to do all the work of the right, and I watched, amazed, as he cut and spliced wires a hell of a lot faster than I could with two good hands. He was a no-nonsense, silent type—and traveled with a no-nonsense black lab, who had no time for Boz. When I asked Charlie the dog's name, he didn't look up from studying a junction box. "Troubles," he said.

We finished work on the house, and with no jobs magically landing at my new doorstep, I grew unhappier. Nora and I started a cycle of arguing, making up, arguing again. I'd been reading Freud, who said that life's a search for love and meaningful work. My lack of the latter was undermining the former, so we agreed that I needed to finish my degree if I hoped to teach, and I wrote a crow-eating letter requesting reinstatement in my grad program. *Hello. Guess who. Just kidding about all that "intolerable, inhumane" stuff. I'd like to come back if it's all right with you.* I hated the idea, but in nine months I'd finish the fucking coursework and return to write my dissertation in the woods. I packed up Boz, kissed Nora good-bye, and retraced my path to Chicago—where I found an oversized attic room in a sprawling Hyde Park house and set to work.

One night, three months later, I was at my desk finishing a paper about dreams in Shelley, that free spirit and no stranger to trouble himself, so I could pack up for Christmas in California— when the phone rang.

"Hello?" I said.

"Hello." Nora. Her voice distant.

"Hi! What's happenin'?"

Pause.

"What is it?" I asked, sensing trouble.

"I've decided . . . that you shouldn't come back for Christmas." Another pause.

"In fact . . . I've decided that you shouldn't come back at all."

"What?" I blurted, snapping upright, a trapdoor swinging open in my stomach.

"Nothing against you. But since I've been alone, I've felt . . . freer . . . more myself than ever in my life. And you know I never liked the idea of marriage."

It's true that I'd more or less talked her into marrying. She'd resisted—until I pointed out that life would easier if she didn't have to hide our living together from her father. A hell of a reason to get married, I know, but we worried about such things in those days. We didn't promise all the "till death do us part" stuff, just to "walk together a while," as long as we could live intensely.

So I know you're thinking that I should have seen it coming. But, a good Minnesota farm boy, I never envisioned the knot coming loose once it was tied. I reasoned and pleaded with her for months, each call leaving my insides ripped open. I quit writing papers, avoided friends, spent days and nights trying to work through my wall of pain. I would've been perfect for Elizabeth Kubler-Ross's research at the U. of C., since I went through her five stages of grief over and over, every fucking week. Well, four stages. I never got to acceptance.

Finally, I wrote Nora I was coming back whether she wanted me to or not, packed Boz into my old Plymouth Valiant, and set out on that long road again—across those interminable plains, that barren Wyoming landscape, Colorado's unforgiving Rockies, Utah's desiccated salt flats, Nevada's scrub deserts—along the way convincing myself that once Nora saw me, love would overcome doubt and we'd make it through these troubles.

Standing again in front of what had once been my house, gleaming white in the bright California afternoon and looking grand from my handiwork, I paused, suddenly uncertain. What did I expect? I'd been a fool to come all this way. I thought of leaving again, but then the door swung open, and there she stood on the top step, as beautiful as ever, her hair blonder, her dancer's legs tan.

"Hello," I said.

"Hello," she returned. "I'm surprised to see you."

"I wrote that I was coming," I said.

"But I didn't really think you would—after I told you not to. Why are you here?"

"Because I love you," I said. "And because I want you back."

She stared at me with those green, green eyes—then shook her head and turned, motioning me toward the front door. Inside, I pleaded, she resisted, we argued, made up, drank wine over dinner and ended up falling into bed together—which, of course, just confused matters worse. A couple days later, she said flatly that I needed to leave. I loaded Boz into the car and was backing out of the yard when I heard Nora call, and jerked up to find her just outside my open window. Hope surged. Would she say it was all a mistake, invite me back in? "Let me know where you end up," she said. "Keep in touch."

In touch? In touch with what? If I'd stayed in touch with her instead of going back to the academic factory, we might still be together. If I'd stayed in touch with myself, with what it took to survive in the world, I might not be in this trouble. I gave a sharp nod and spat gravel as I dropped down the drive. Around a bend in the deserted road, I stopped, letting the car idle as the realization hit me with stomach-sinking force.

I was homeless.

Homeless? Me? I couldn't believe it. Looking back on it now, I see that I hadn't really traveled very far up the Taxonomy of Troubles; but in that moment, having gone looking for trouble and finding trouble of a different kind, I was desperate, despairing. Where was my shining future of freedom, of madness?

For the next week or so, I wandered Sonoma County in a daze, from the ocean, apt emblem of my own vast emptiness, inland to Petaluma, where I'd wash up at a park and head to a bakery for coffee and a donut—trying to make my dwindling money last. Leaving this place—so wrapped up with love and my dreams of Nora and freedom—was admitting defeat. No, I needed to stay—which meant getting a roof over my head and a job. Finally, I thought of Charlie, the only person I knew with a house *and* steady work.

When Charlie's pickup chugged into view that evening, I was sitting on the front porch of his tiny house. As he caught sight of me, I gave a friendly wave. He nodded without waving back, parked, crawled out, and curled an arm under Troubles's belly, easing him to the ground. "Hi, Charlie," I said, a bit too brightly, as he approached.

"Hi," he said, wiping sweat from his forehead with his chopped hand. "What's up?"

Trying not to sound pitiful with a man who'd known much more trouble than mine, I worked my way through the tale of Nora, of sleeping in the car, and all, finally getting to my need for a place to crash—temporarily, mind you, just until I could get my feet under me. "I'm used to living alone," he said at the end, his tone flat. As if on cue, a bark and yelp, and we snapped around to see Boz lurching back from Charlie's lab. "Troubles is used to living alone, too," Charlie said. "Not sure they'd get along."

"Oh, Boz is just friendly, is all. I'll keep him away, don't you worry."

Inside, over beers at his small kitchen table, he finally agreed. "OK," he said. "But I don't expect you'll be staying long." I still have no idea why he took in a sorry piece of horse dooky like me. Maybe his own troubles let him see mine. Anyway, I had a roof over my head again, and for the next couple of weeks, I spent evenings trying to stay out of Charlie's way, days roaming the county trying to scare up work. I found nothing, and as time passed, Charlie's irritation grew. One night, getting ready for yet another meal where I hadn't contributed anything, I watched from the kitchen table as he stood silently at the counter, anchoring a carrot on the cutting board with the heel of his bad hand while he wielded a long, wide knife with the other. "Can I help?" I asked.

"No," came the brusque reply. And just then, the carrot leaped as if alive across the kitchen floor and rolled to my feet. I picked it up and held it out to him. "You sure?" I said, thinking, *Hey, I've got two good hands. Why can't you let me do something for you? Let me be useful.* He snatched the carrot, ran it quickly under the tap, and went back to the task. He didn't say a word, but I seemed to hear his voice, which came as my own. *What the fuck are you waiting for, man? You've got two good hands and a whole world in front of you. Just get on with your goddamned life.*

I suddenly saw myself as that person Faulkner talks about who clings to trouble because he's "more afraid of the trouble he might have than he ever is of the trouble he's already got." My pride and my vague dreams were, I saw now, simple vanity. With Nora gone from my life, there was nothing left for me in California. Chicago would at least offer connections that might help me find a path. If Charlie could make it through what had come his way, I had no excuse not to take charge of my fate. When I told him, he just nodded like he'd known all along the thing that I couldn't see right before my eyes. Even Troubles, sensing that Boz and I were soon out of his life, suddenly turned friendly.

The next morning, I headed east again.

A teacher for three decades now, all these years later I often end the semester with a poem by the great Sufi poet, Hafiz. In Daniel Ladinsky's wonderful translation from *The Gift*, it's called "Just Looking for Trouble," and it tells of a student who would sit alone in his house at night "Shivering with worries / And fears" until one day his teacher crafts a knife from him that helps him lose his fears. Since then, he says, not only has that student lost all his fear, "Now he goes out / Just looking for / Trouble."

The main task, I tell my students, is not to stay out of trouble, but to find the *right kind* of trouble. Sometimes, you get more than you'd bargained for—sometimes, like Charlie, a lot more—but if you manage to work through it, you're maybe a little more alive, and a little readier when the biggest trouble comes at the end to say, as a friend who died recently said with his last words, "It's all good."

Of course, I knew nothing of that then. As I made my way through the back roads of Sonoma County and across California on my way to the Sierra Nevadas, with Boz standing on the backseat, his head on my shoulder growing heavier with each mile as if he sensed the yawning feeling of failure in the depths of my being, I was not yet ready to glean any lesson from my experience. I did not yet know that lessons, if they come at all, generally emerge only after we have passed through our trouble. In mid-November, with winter approaching and only enough money in my pocket for gas and a little food, the states rolled by in a blur—Nevada, Utah, Colorado, Wyoming, Nebraska—and I felt no freedom in being on the road, giving myself over instead to self-pity as I replayed images of Nora, of our house, of my failed California dream mile after dreary mile. And even after I arrived at my parents' farm three hellish days later, borrowed some money, and crawled back into Chicago to begin grad school and work four part-time jobs to survive while Boz and I fought for kibble, I still didn't know what it all meant.

Even today, decades later, I'm not sure. I can't claim that I've always found the right kind of trouble since those long-ago California days. Like most folks, I have been through the whole cycle of troubles and triumphs and troubles time and again. But I'vVe pushed through—had some luck, too—and ended up with a wonderful daughter, a wonderful woman, great friends, a life of telling stories, and the privilege and joy of teaching. And while I left California, I did manage to keep the dream—of freedom, of movement, of the wildness that keeps us dancing through life's minefield of troubles. And maybe, in the end, that's all I really should have expected. 🪑

A PROSTITUTE COMPARISON

BY MOLLY EACH

I'm in the front row at this live sex show in Amsterdam and this woman is sprawled across the stage, spread-eagle, putting a candle into her . . . *you know*. Then she lights it. Anyone can do that, right? But then she proceeds to do all sorts of acrobatics, flipping from her back to her front, rolling over her love handles on each side, her legs twisting around her head, moving like a roll of pretzel dough being shaped, the candle remaining firmly inside her and her inner thighs remaining unscorched. She finishes her tumbling routine, tilts her head, blows out the candle with a wink, and exits the stage. The crowd of mostly tourists claps approvingly, and a few guys in the back whoop loudly. But me? All I can 'think about is how my shoulder is touching Brian's right now, making my stomach flip from the back to the front, and how just a second ago—before she lit the candle—he was rubbing his hand up and down my thigh and how now my body is tingling just from being near him, although I can't tell if that's lust or the fact that I'm high out of my mind.

The summer after my sophomore year in college, I backpacked around Europe for two months with Youssef, Tim, and Alek—three of my guy friends from high school. At twenty years old, I was a prim, polished, good-as-gold Minnesotan. I knew how to have fun and all, but in my early college days, fun involved playing board games, making dinners, and sucking down Amaretto sours—a routine that sidestepped the sex, drugs, and all-night parties of my college peers. I'd tried weed twice before, and both times I'd giggled, eaten my body weight in Cheetos, passed out, and found myself unable to put together a coherent sentence for days after. I decided it wasn't my thing.

As for the sex, well, um, I was practically a virgin. I'd dated one guy in high school and two guys in college, but we could never seem to round third base before a major relationship flaw was revealed. I'd finally done it with this guy I was casually seeing a few months before my trip, but it was kind of lame, full of awkward silences and words like "Oops!" and "Oh, sorry." And I'd only seen two pornos, totaling a combined three-and-a-half minutes. The first, an up-close view of penetration, courtesy of my friend Jay Brown, who popped it on television at a party in high school; the second, a few minutes of an orgy when we accidentally got an X-rated channel for five minutes my freshman year of college. And I'd never experienced one of those horrific walk-in-on-mom-and-dad incidents, and never came home to my roommates knockin' boots with their boyfriends on the couch. My closest "yikes" moment was walking in on my college roommate Becky masturbating, and the awkwardness that followed was enough to sour me on ever seeing anyone experience, um, genital pleasure again.

So how did a twenty-year-old half-virgin with minimal drug history end up sitting at a live sex show in Amsterdam high as a fucking kite? One word: Brian.

Brian was not who I expected to meet on my European odyssey. I wanted to be swept off my feet by a stunning Parisian, a macho Spaniard, or a German beefcake. I wanted a do-over on my first time—I wanted to kill my virginity in style, to have memories of sex on a deserted Mediterranean beach, the salty wind whipping my hair, or to be whisked away on horseback to a secluded hotel in the Alps and have my first time surrounded by candles in a plush, 500-year-old bed made by Austrian monks. I wanted to come back with stories for my friends. I wanted to look longingly out the window as we sipped glasses of wine. I wanted to say things like, "This Bordeaux reminds me of Pierre and the Eiffel Tower" or, "Spätzle? You haven't had spätzle until you've eaten it off of Klaus's pecs."

But things hadn't played out the way I wanted. Parisian stunners, macho Spaniards, and German beefcakes had all eluded me, aside from the occasional drunken conversation and a few awkward public transportation feel-ups. So by the time we showed up in Amsterdam in week four, I had resigned myself: a European romance was just not in my cards.

We arrived in the afternoon, dropped off our bags and locked them to poles in our forty-bed hostel room, and walked through the streets of Amsterdam, the beautiful public art and colorful architecture blending with neon-lit hash bars. Dying for their first legal marijuana experience, Youssef, Tim, and Alek led me into the Grasshopper, a clean and kinda glitzy hash bar across the street. With sunbeams reflecting off the silver tables, a counter full of neatly organized marijuana to choose from and a friendly staff who guided us through our purchase, smoking weed seemed elegant and refined—something Grace Kelly or Princess Diana would indulge in. With my friends' gentle encouragement, and their cross-their-hearts promises that they wouldn't let anything bad happen to me (or let me near any Cheetos), I dug in, taking puff after puff as my friends circulated several varieties around our crew. With every hit, the sun seemed to shine brighter, Youssef, Tim, and Alek glowed like angels, and my body felt so light it felt like I was my own shadow. Yeah, I know. It was crazy.

Sufficiently baked, a huge grin stapled to my face, we moved to a table on the Grasshopper's outdoor patio. A strange, busy calm washed over us as we sat in super-high silence, each lost on our own buzzy worlds. A crew of five guys in dirty T-shirts and Converse All-Stars walked b, and, recognizing us as Americans, pulled a table up next to ours. The guys made conversation while I zoned out, watching the throngs of people on the sidewalk and trying to pick out who else was totally high (which is a really awesome game in Amsterdam, when Brian walked up to our table. It was like out of a movie, I swear! "Dream Weaver" played in the background, and the world around him got blurry as his cargo pants swayed in slow-motion. I stared, unable to avert my small, bloodshot eyes

"You guys got started without me, I see?" he said to his friends, then smiled and walked around the table towards me, where, in one fluid motion, he scooped up a chair from the table next to us, nudged his friend to move over, and positioned himself right next to me. He stuck out his hand. "Hey. I'm Brian."

"Hi," I said, trying to be cute, though it felt like my mouth was stuffed with gauze. "I'm Molly."

Now, normally Brian's type would have totally turned me off, as I was super into tall, ugly alternative rockers who had less body fat than me (think Thom Yorke from Radiohead), and Brian looked like a Backstreet Boy. Spiky, gel-laden hair, über-chees, frayed cargo pants, a popped-collar polo shirt, and an aura of slightly nauseating CK One cologne, but still, my stomach did one of those awesome leaps of joy when he sat down next to me. I think it was his eyes this light sapphire color and his ear-to-ear smile with shimmering white teeth. If I had passed him on the street I wouldn't have given him a second look, but with his body turned towards mine, radiating tension and heat and sex mere inches away, suddenly the popped collar and gelled hair were easy to ignore.

With the touch of my arm he engaged me in conversation, and the typical where-are-you-from, where-have-you-traveled, evolved into talk of our families, our friends, and a shared love of Barcelona and Minnesota Timberwolves power forward Kevin Garnett. At one point, he paused and rubbed the small of my back. It made my entire body tingle! "An adorable American girl who likes Garnett? I never thought I'd find that in Amsterdam." I smiled shyly, feeling my cheeks flush, the oncoming crush making me dizzy. Even through my baked haze, I couldn't believe how well we were getting along! He was funny, smart, kind, and a wonderful dose of comfort in this strange land. After several more joints, our group decided it was time to explore the Red Light District. Brian held my hand and stayed close to my side as we veered into the heart of this notorious neighborhood.

The Red Light District is a crazy, X-rated circus. People are moving fast yet slow, their voices echoing through the streets, floating across the bridges and canals. Prostitutes mill around in storefront windows, like lingerie-clad Victoria's Secret mannequins come to life. Everything is so full of bright neon colors, there's constant cheesy Euro-pop music playing in the background of every establishment, and you're just getting glimpses of sex everywhere: fornicating couples on the covers of DVDs through the wide open doors of porn shops; extreme close-ups of body parts on sex show advertisements. In my marijuana haze, I stared at every scantily-clad prostitute, writhing in her display window; I gawked at every guy who came out of their dens; I stopped to hear every seedy guy's list of available drugs over and over, their chants of, "Pot, pills, X, LSD," ringing in my brain. In my high amazement, I would have gotten lost along those streets, like *really* lost, if it weren't for Brian. While the guys walked ahead, Brian stayed with m , holding my hand. He bought me a rose from a street vendor, and ran for a bottle of water when I mentioned I had cotton mouth. He was attentive and sweet, even glancing over at the prostitutes, who stared at him behind their windows, then looking back at me and saying, "They're not as hot as you."

I know, right? It's cheesy and lame. But it makes sense: if your European lover is French, he may call you *mon petit chou*, or if he's Spanish he might woo you with wine and a sultry Flamenco dance. But if he's an American in Amsterdam, it's going to be a prostitute comparison, and based on the number of dudes who stood around the windows drooling and counting their money, it totally worked. I was smitten.

"Hey! Let's go to a live sex show!" yelled Tim. Our crew had stopped in front of a dark entryway. Outside was a sandwich board about as tall as me that rea, "LIVE SEX!" in bright red, bubble letters

A small, round guy stood outside holding a wad of money, looking very much like Sonny from *The Godfather*. "Seventy," he said.

"Um, dollars?" I asked.

"Yup, seventy dollars. But girls get in free." I couldn't help but smile at him. He ignored me, hand outstretched, while the guys dug around in their wallets and added to the man's huge cash pile. I looked up at Brian and smiled, and we held hands as the two of us headed down the stairs into a dark basement that vaguely reeked of vinegar, musk, and sweat. A few red lights dangled from the ceiling (highlighting Brian's awesome bone structure), and around a smallish stage were three sections of chairs in a U-shape, and all fifty of them would be full before the show started. I followed the guys as we filed into our seats, which I'm sure where coated with a million STDs, and which were in the very front, or what Youssef, Tim, and Ale — all strip club veterans–referred to as "sniffer's row," which made me want to yak. I sat next to Brian, of course, who put his arm around me and pulled me close. "Don't be nervous," he whispered, his hot breath lingering in my ear. I curled up next to him.

As the lights went down, and the stage illuminated with a small overhanging lamp (and Brian held me closer), a lovely tall and lean Latina in a string bikini walked onto the scuffed wooden stage. She called for a volunteer. I looked around the crowd to see who would raise his hand, and noticed a tall, burly dude across the room practically leap out of his seat. He joined her on stage, where the Latina pulled off his shirt, peeled off her bikini bottom, and ordered him to lie down on his back. My eyes were as big as basketballs as she pulled a big fat magic marker out of her bikini top and put it—uncapped—into her vag, much like her candle-wielding friend, who would take the stage next. As samba music played in the background, she squatted down so she was a foot over the burly guy's chest and began to grind. She circled her hips softly yet certainly, moving them around and back again, circling them over the guy, who lay like a mummy, though you could see that his hands were itching to at least touch her, as she just kept bumping and grinding and circling and pulsing.

Suddenly, she stopped, stood up, and pulled the burly dude into a standing position. She motioned to his chest, "Ta-da!" she said. In black magic marker, written in huge letters from his collarbone to his belly button were the words, "I love you." He glowed, the audience clapped, and I looked at Brian and tried to hide my smile. I knew this *must* have been a sign. I mean, we were at a live sex show—the word love wasn't even supposed to be in the building, much less broadcast across the stage! I was giddy. Maybe I'd not only get my European romance, but perhaps Brian was destined to be much more! My stoned mind flashed a vision of our friends and families throwing rice in our direction as we drove away from a church, tin cans clanking loudly from the bumper of the car as he moved my veil away from my face, and we kissed. I sighed in the dark club. It would be so beautiful

The stage illuminated again to reveal the candle woman, followed by a couple dressed in ninja outfits who fought each other before stripping each other's clothes off and fucking in about fifty different positions before she finished on top and then killed him. It was weird. "That dude wasn't even hard," Brian said. "It was totally fake." I smiled back, but I was too busy looking at/touching/ thinking about Brian to even care. The way his hair glowed in the light, the slightly amused smile he had on his face, the way he put his arm around me—I fell into a daydream where he carried me over-the-threshold style out of the sex show, to a gorgeous room at the Ritz Amsterdam where we would have sex in sixty different positions, and he would totally be hard the whole time, and it would be amazing.

The sound of pounding bongo drums woke me out of my fantasy, and suddenly there was an enormous 300-pound woman, with a fruit-decorated Chiquita banana-style wrap on her head and a two-piece yellow bikini, making her way down the aisle. She shook her enormous breasts all around the room. She carried a basket of bananas that she held on her hip, occasionally putting one into her cleavage and then presenting it to an audience member to take out as she shook wildly. Taking her place on stage, she promptly stripped and called for a volunteer. I peered around the room, waiting for some other tourist to raise their hand, when I felt the side of my body shift slightly.

"Me!" Brian shouted. He shot up, arm raised and started walking towards the stage. He briefly glanced back at me with an "I fucking rule" smile and made his way to the stage

Brian unpeeled a banana at the request of the woman–smiling this shit-eating grin at our group the entire time–and she took it and lay down. Then she stuck the banana inside of her and spread her legs. She motioned at Brian, like, "Come here," then pointed right at her crotch. He knelt down without hesitating for a moment, pulled her legs apart even farther, and began to eat the banana. No joke, he just chewed away, taking bite after bite, going closer and closer to her vag. My front row angle meant I was just a few feet away from the action, and had an up-close view of his head bobbing up and down. The music wasn't nearly as loud as it should have been, because I could hear the gross chomping and chewing of a banana being eaten a nasty enough sound under *normal* circumstances.

The audience whooped and hollered, Brian kept eating, and I just stared at him, wondering if there were magic mushrooms mixed in with my marijuana. Every three bites or so, he'd come up onto his knees, raise his arms victoriously, finish chewing, then head down for more. At the end, just as he was headed into dangerous territory, the enormous woman reached around, grabbed the back of his spiky, blond hair, pushed it into her crotch, and rubbed it around for a solid twenty seconds. Then the lights went down. The crowd sat in a stunned silence for a moment before Brian's friends, who sat down the row from me, broke the quiet with loud, approving cheers. The rest of the audience followed suit. I just sat and stared at the dingy ground.

When they came back up, Brian was on his feet, that same expression of "I fucking rule" visible underneath the smeared banana, thick clear spit, and whatever else clung to his mouth and chin. He made a show of licking his lips, then wiping the remainder of the smudge from his mouth with his sleeve. He ran off the stage, pumping his fists like a track star, slapped high-fives with his friends and sat down next to me, pushing his body next to mine as it had been before.

"Wow, that was sweet!" he said, putting his arm around me again. "What did you think?" He stared right at me, and all I could smell was sour banana. Bits of it still lingered on his cheeks and in the corners of his mouth, and when I looked closely, it was starting to crust over. "Cool, huh?" He waited for my response.

"Um, it was . . . " I didn't know how to answer. "Something," I finally said.

We filed out of our seats, up the stairs, and emerged into the fresh air and chaos of the Red Light District. Brian grabbed my hand for a moment and turned me to him. "So what's up now? You know, I've got a single hostel room," he whispered, moving closer, bending his head towards mine. The sour banana smell was more pungent now, and I could practically see the syphilis dancing around on his mouth.

I stepped back and stuck out my hand. "Nice to meet you, Brian," I said. He took a step closer, looking confused, and I reached down, shook his hanging arm, and let it drop. "I hope you have a nice trip." I walked through the Red Light District towards my hostel, finally feeling un-high. I pictured Brian standing still, confused, a Backstreet Boy abandoned among the lingerie-clad prostitutes, chants of "pot, pills, X, LSD," high tourists, fornicating couples, bottled water vendors, and Sonny Corleone and his giant stack of money. This time, the sex and drugs failed to fascinate me. Instead, it was seedy and gross, like the whole thing had taken on the sheen of smeared banana liquid. I walked further away from my familiar American dude, not turning once to gawk or stare at anything, amazed that among this neighborhood of filth that a Backstreet Boy American could stand out as the most disgusting thing of all. For the rest of the trip, when I lay in bed and thought about finally losing my virginity for real, I didn't see Klaus, or Pierre, or any sort of random Americans. Suddenly, the story I wanted to tell my friends involved a sweetly predictable Minnesota boy in a normal bed

And, while we're at it, no food.

COUNTING DAYS
BY BOBBY BIEDRZYCKI

So this past October I celebrated one year of continuous sobriety. That means right now, I'm about 446 days, twenty-two hours, and fourteen minutes sober. Give or take a few seconds. Don't worry, this doesn't make me some kind of informant for the sober police, you can all keep drinking. It just means that I'm in recovery, and in recovery we have this saying that "the dark past is the greatest possession we have." It means basically that, as addicts, we can't forget where we came from. We can't forget what we were like, what happened, and what we are like now.

My dark past started with whiskey at age twelve, crack cocaine by sixteen, and eventually heroin. I existed in the dark past for almost twenty years, and then, it got worse.

Two months before I got sober I came to one morning at the Chicago Transit Authority's 95th Street Red Line station. I was huddled in a corner near the turnstiles, caked in dirt from head to toe. I had been having these massive anxiety attacks, and the medication for those combined with the drinking had started causing me to black out and lose large periods of time, mostly hours, sometimes days. That morning, at the train station, I was crouched over hugging my knees, rocking back and forth like an autistic child, panhandling for change with a Styrofoam cup.

A month later, I went out to get drunk with friends and woke up in the hospital as my stomach was being pumped. I turned and vomited into the nurse's face. They released me from the emergency room the next morning and I wore my identification bracelet around like a badge of honor. Publicly, I was so proud to be a drunk. Privately, I was scared shitless. I went home and cried myself to sleep.

In the weeks leading up to my sober date, I had been keeping an active list in my journal of the things I wanted to include in my suicide letter. I made a deal with myself that if I could get nothing else right in this world, I would at least succeed in writing this letter. I wanted to do things like absolve my family and friends from guilt and make sure specific pieces of my horror memorabilia collection went to certain people.

The dark past was quickly becoming pitch black.

A concerned friend begged me to try a meeting. "Fine," I told her. "I will go to one meeting. Just one." The words were eerily similar to the refrain I used to use before walking in a bar: just one.

Twelve Hours Sober: I go to my first meeting. It's in a hospital, and I have to walk around the building three times before I decide to enter the sliding glass doors. I sit quietly in a corner seat and speak to no one. But the moment I walk out, I know I have to go back. The next day, I find one in an abandoned storefront on North Avenue. But the one you need to know about, the one where I first encounter Mick, is in the basement of a church. The place is packed: fifty, maybe sixty people. I'm a few days sober, and I still have the shakes. Mick is the lead speaker, a small but muscular ex-city employee in his 50s from the North Side of Chicago. I sense immediately that he could kick my ass, and this is important to me. I don't know why. When the meeting ends he walks over and offers me his phone number.

I pretend to put it into my phone and he asks if I want to go get coffee. We sit in a small coffee shop on an anonymous corner in Chicago and talk about addiction. It's 9 p.m. and raining heavily outside. Mick smiles a lot and swears even more and often looks at the asses of various women who enter the shop. Cars splash by, and I tell him that sitting and drinking coffee after a meeting makes me feel like an alcoholic cliché, He laughs and asks me what waking up in my own vomit made me feel like?

I'm silent.

I begin to go to meetings with other addicts on a daily basis. The rooms are small and large. They're filled with doctors, lawyers, moms, dads, prostitutes, and airplane pilots. People talk. People listen. People laugh. People cry. They are happening all over the city. (Odds are one is taking place right now.) I realize that I've been walking past them for years unaware of their existence.

Fourteen Days Sober: We sit in the same coffee shop, and I formally ask Mick to be my sponsor. He tells me yes, and then he leans in over his coffee and states the conditions, his stubby callused index finger hitting the table each time he wants to accentuate a point. "You call every day no matter what. You go to meetings. You work the steps."

Forty-two Days Sober: We sit in a different coffee shop; this one is on a college campus, and students study at the tables around us. Mick asks me if the anxiety attacks have stopped. They have, kind of. But I tell him now I constantly feel bombarded by liquor advertisements. They come at me from storefront windows, all neon and smiles, or the huge billboards of glistening drinks, condensation slowly spilling down the glasses threaten to swallow me up. But the worst are the doors of the dive bars. The front doors of the dark, windowless bars I used to crawl into and hide inside for days. Anytime I pass one, the urge to push the door open, jump on a stool, and order a vodka rocks is almost unbearable. Sometimes I have to cross the street just to get away from them.

Mick asks if I'm praying, and this is where we hit the wall. Higher power, praying—the words alone make my skin crawl. I want to lie. I want to walk out. I want to drink. But instead, I try something different, I tell the truth.

"I don't believe in God," I tell Mick. "So that makes praying kind of tough."

"That's okay," he says. "Did you ever believe in anything?"

"I dunno, I guess when I was a kid." I tell him about Catholic school and the horrible things that happened there and how I begged God for them to stop but they didn't, so fuck God. God is for the weak-minded, science is what I believe in, and he lets me go on and on for nearly a half hour. Then he stands up and gives me a hug, and we both start to cry.

Another man from our meeting walks into the shop and says, "See, this is what it's all about right here: two big, burly guys huggin' it the fuck out." We stop hugging each other, and laugh. Then we each give this man a hug.

In those hugs, I feel it.

I begin to meditate. Calling it mediation makes me feel better. "Praying" is hard for me to say out loud. The disease would rather think of it as praying though, because the disease would prefer that I close my mind, hold onto my old perceptions of things. Hold on to my ego. The disease knows these perceptions; it believes this ego will eventually lead me back to using and ultimately to death.

I tell Mick it's hard to meditate. He says start for five seconds. Just ask God to keep you sober and go about your day. I still cannot say the word "God," but I don't tell him this. When I leave the coffee shop I can feel my disease rumbling deep inside me, shape shifting, smiling, winning. The liquor signs and bar doors are particularly hard to pass.

Sixty-eight Days Sober: The anxiety begins to build. Mick, my friends, other addicts in the program tell me over and over again that it's not about God, not about the word "God," or the religious aspect, it's about willingness. The willingness to say I don't know everything, the willingness to smash my own ego, to say maybe, just maybe there is something bigger than me, even if I can't define what it is. The willingness to start over. To be reborn. I cry at night. Twice in one week I walk into dive bars and leave without ordering.

Seventy-two Days Sober: Another program member approaches me in that same church basement. He is tall and thin, and I have never noticed him before this moment. Earlier in the meeting, I was rambling on about my inability to pray and meditate. He suggests that I pray in Arabic: "*lâ ilâha illâ allâh.*" He tells me it means, "There is no God, but God." I ask him to write it down for me.

I try it the next morning: *lâ ilâha illâ allâh*. There is no God, but God.

I say it five times.

Then I start to say it every day and soon after, I'm not exactly sure when, the bar doors get easier and easier to pass, until eventually I don't even notice them.

Two-hundred Five Days Sober: Mick and I sit in Dunkin' Donuts. It's hard work, I tell him, staying clean, talking to God, rebuilding everything in your world. He tells me to get my thoughts off that shit and onto today, day two hundred five.

He looks me right in the eyes, fiercely and sincerely: "What're you gonna do today to save your life?" he asks, and then we both get up and walk over to the church basement. And keep counting. 🏛

RETURN TRIP

BY PATRICIA ANN McNAIR

Ok, so we're on our way to Northern Michigan, me and Philip—my now husband, my then boyfriend—and it's the late summer of 2003. And we turn off the interstate and there it is, the sound. The car is definitely talking. "Hit the radio," I tell Philip, and he does. Yup, that damn sound is still there. Like the radio turned low and badly tuned. A whispering under the wheels. Ghosts.

We're on our way to Glen Arbor, where we are going to share a residency, me and Philip, him doing his painting and printmaking, me, my writing. My writing that—since our last trip up north, and with the wedding and funeral and moving and, shit, plain old city life—seems to work just like this car: more rattle and noise than anything else.

Our last time here in Northern Michigan in 2001, I was teaching-writer-in-residence at Interlochen, a small arts boarding school deep in the woods and far away from the city. Philip was with me. Or, I thought he was with me. On the way up, though, he said something like, "I may not stay here very long."

"Here?" I said. "Here, here—you know, the United States," he's British, by the way—"*here* here? or here, Interlochen?"

"Here," he said. "Um, Interlochen. Here." We were sort of living together then. Trying it out, even though he still had a foot in London, had a show opening there, would be going back and forth.

"Oh," I said, or maybe, "Sure, fine, whatever."

Asshole, I must have thought. Protecting myself, of course. But still, he came with me then in 2001, he and my fat black cat, the real love of my life, Rafiki.

So it was 2001, like I said, right? And the first day of classes was September 11, 2001. September 11. 2001. I didn't have a television in my tiny, two-room cabin, so I heard about what happened in New York, in D.C., and in that field in the middle of the country when I got to school. And after I'd heard, I walked into the girls' bathroom and found one of my students there. She was sobbing, trembling, hyperventilating. Her face was white and wet.

"I have to talk to my parents," she said. Her parents were teaching in Qatar, and the girl couldn't get through on the phone. "My father," she said and gulped for breath. I patted her back, stroked her hair. "My mother."

Later that day in my cabin that smelled like summer camp—mold, wet pine needles, bug spray—I called my own mother, home in Evanston. And on her answering machine, her voice was distant, shaky. She'd made the recording after we'd got the diagnosis. Before I could start to worry, I remembered that it was Tuesday. Chemo day. She'd be at the hospital.

So on our return trip in 2003, our car rattles its way through Manistee, a Victorian port town on the scenic route up North. I always preferred this route that runs near the lake to the other way that takes you up through the boring palm of Michigan. On damp days, the sky on this side gets misty over the trees, romantic-looking. It's hot today, though, and clear. The goddamn car makes a sound.

And again, I turn off the air conditioner. The noise doesn't stop but the windows fog up, so I turn it back on again.

Outside of Manistee on Route 31, the car is really rumbling.

"Turn the radio back on," Philip says, like maybe if we can't hear it, it will go away, problem solved, like maybe if you pretend it's not there, it won't be. Good plan. I get it. I hit the button. What was on? "Radar Love," maybe, driving us forward, pushing us to where we want so desperately to be, the song's percussion and the rumble adding urgency to the trip.

On September 15, 2001, there were no planes flying from Cherry Capital Airport, so Philip stood on line at the bus station with the late summer tourists and students and salesmen. He was due back in London for a gallery opening, so he'd take the crowded bus to Chicago where he'd wait to catch a flight back to the place that was still sort of home for him.

A few days after that, I drove home to visit my mother. She was battling stage IV lung cancer, and I dreaded all that was to come, but that drive alone in my car on that September day was spectacular. The road was a dark vein with the trees beside it going red, going gold, going orange, and it all stunned me. The gentle slope of land and the curve of the highway as it passed close to Lake Michigan and through those small towns was almost too much to bear. I cried most of the way.

Chemotherapy was to enhance my mother's quality of life, the doctor said. That was the best we could hope for since the disease was inoperable and incurable. *Terminal*, they meant, though no one said it. Four months had passed since we discovered what the back pain and cracked ribs and labored breathing had been caused by, and this new mixture of drugs had had a good effect on her. Her breathing was easier, she was in better spirits, less pain, and the tumor had even gotten smaller. She had her favorite nieces come to stay with her, one after the other, while I, her only daughter, ran off to another state for five months. Still, we talked every day.

"How you doing, Mom?"

"Good," she'd say, and mean it most times, I could tell even from so far away, even from my hiding place in the woods. I imagined her in her favorite chair with a game of solitaire on her lapboard in front of her, smiling into the phone. Her smile my smile.

"How are you, darlin'?"

"Good," I'd say.

"Good," she'd say.

"Good," I'd say.

"Good."

She came to visit on Parents' Weekend, her last trip anywhere. She'd been a travel writer most of her life, always happiest on the road, so she understood why I'd left. Now I wanted to show off to her, read her the dozens of pages I'd been able to write in the quiet, to walk with her over my running path through the wetlands. I wanted her to love as I did the little cabin I lived in with Philip—when he wasn't off in London or somewhere—and with my cat Rafiki. But she was sick that weekend, her head and lungs thick with cold. I drove her to Sleeping Bear Dunes to look at the great lake and see the changing leaves, and she slept in the front seat beside me, snoring softly, her wig slightly askew under her hat, missing the bright yellow trees against the blue sky, the crimson weeds standing roadside. She'd grown up in Vermont, and I wanted her to see a real autumn one more time, but she didn't wake up, and I couldn't help but think, as I drove through the woods, that this is how things look when they begin to die.

On our way to Glen Arbor in 2003, Route 31 takes us into pretty Bear Lake, where we'll stop for gas and hope that the car starts up again. I can feel it rumbling harder under the floorboards. At the gas station with a view, Philip is enamored with the shimmering lake again, drawn into the memory of this place.

On one of our other trips to Michigan, I drove him through

this town and showed him my dream house, a rambling Victorian with a wide lawn directly across the highway from Bear Lake. It was for sale. Philip called it "Patty's House," and he took a picture of me on its lawn. In the photo, the house looms white and huge behind me, and I'm staring out past the camera not quite smiling, like there's something that is or isn't there.

Full of gas the car starts—*yes!*—but the noise is bigger now, like a truck. No, more like a semi. So I don't even see the house when we pass, or the lake at our side either. My eyes are on the road, what's ahead, what I want to—no, *need* to—get to tonight, tonight, tonight. A cabin. The woods. I am willing the car to make it, please make it. And I know that this might be considered praying by some, that sort of praying that those of us do even if we don't really believe in prayer. *Please make it*, I say in my head. *Please make it. Don't die don't die don't die don't die.*

On the last day of Parents' Weekend, Rafiki got sick. He'd crouch in a corner and growl, or find a warm spot in the sun on the carpet and curl into a black heap. He wouldn't eat. When my mom left, I took him to the vet. No big deal, it seemed, a urinary tract infection. Cats get 'em all the time; they kept him for a few days. Philip came back again, and we brought Rafiki home to the cabin with a big, expensive bag of special food that he wouldn't eat. The vet suggested baby food, but that didn't interest Rafiki either.

"Don't worry," the vet said, "he'll eat when he's ready."

She was a dog person, I could tell. She didn't know shit about cats. Cats do things their own damn way. Cat don't want to eat, a cat don't eat. Shit. Cat people know this.

Philip left again, and Rafiki took a turn for the worse. He barely moved, he still wasn't eating, and he stopped drinking water. I wrapped him in a towel and took him to a different vet, no more dog vet for him, and she felt under his ribs, asked questions, checked his eyes and ears and vitals and said that he had a mass in his abdomen.

They took x-rays and it looked like his liver, like maybe a tumor. Exploratory surgery, she suggested. And you know how it is: when someone you love is ill, you try anything.

It turned out to be fatty liver disease, often brought on when a fat cat stops eating. Those damn dog vets. And I found myself searching the Internet for information, just like I'd done when they named Mom's cancer. It didn't have to be fatal, most said, but it often was. The vet suggested a feeding tube, stitched into the stomach so he'd be less likely to vomit. I had to go home for Thanksgiving, the last one I would get to celebrate with my family as I knew it, and so I visited Rafiki before I left. The young woman vet had given the case to her superior, a quiet man with eyebrows so blond they disappeared. He was soft-spoken, but told you everything, good and bad. My mom's oncologist was a quiet man, too. He'd stroke his upper lip and consider long before answering our questions. And when he didn't have good news about her illness, he would tell my mom and me about his family. His son was in middle school. His daughter was very musical. And on the way home from the cancer center, Mom and I talked about him; how does he have time to have a family? He always answered our pages, even in the middle of the night when Mom was fevered and throwing up, when she was too scared to let me go home until we called him and he told her that it would be okay, it was just a side effect of the chemo. "Take an analgesic," he'd say. "You'll feel better in the morning." She usually did.

The chief vet gave me his home phone number since it was a holiday weekend, and I left Rafiki, his belly shaved and wrapped in an Ace bandage. He trembled and stared at me from his cage, his golden eyes wide. He was terrified, I was terrified, and yet, (there's a pattern here) I left. And I went home to my stronger—but still dying—mother.

I came back to Interlochen a day earlier than planned after our family Thanksgiving, my chest aching from the leaving and from what I had to return to. I would pick up Rafiki and continue the tube feeding myself, even though it didn't seem to be working at the vet's.

"Sometimes it helps to be home," the vet said.

So I brought Rafiki back to our cabin home where we'd be alone. Philip was in London again, and everyone on campus was still gone for the holiday. After I'd give Rafiki his medicine through the feeding tube, he'd hobble across my writing table to push his forehead against a small, pearly boulder Philip had found on a walk in the woods. Head pressing, they call this; I'd read about it on the Internet. Animals sometimes do it when their livers are diseased. Think how often we all do it, push our head against something, feel the steady comfort of something solid. You know, like when you were a kid and you'd turn your face into the skirt of your mother, lean your head against the flesh and muscle underneath.

Philip called regularly during all of this, but he was so far away.

"Things are happening here," he'd say about his art, his show. "This might not be the right time to move."

"Oh," I'd say, "I see." My cat was dying. My mother was dying. I held the phone tighter in my hand. Soon I would be alone.

By now you're probably wondering why the hell would I want to come back to this place. Cats die here. Like Rafiki did when I couldn't save him, when I took him back to the vet to put him to rest. Mothers and boyfriends live hundreds, thousands of miles away. But here it is 2003 again, and our car is rattling toward Honor, and we pass that crazy place with the cartoon character lawn ornaments that flank a sign that says "Jesus died for us." Behind the display is a house with a sagging front porch. The closest neighbors are at least a mile away.

A man moves out to the country and no one is around for miles—this is the way an old joke starts. He gets invited by a grizzly, dirty old neighbor guy to a party. Have you heard this? You know how it goes, I'll give you a short version: "There'll be drinking; there'll be fighting; there'll be fucking." Yadda yadda. Right? "What should I wear?" the new guy asks. "Don't matter," the neighbor says. "It'll just be the two of us."

Loneliness, my friends, is a scary thing. But here's what I know now: it can be a good thing, too, being alone in the woods in a two room cabin with snow outside and black squirrels like ink blots on white, and you're so far away from the noise of the city where planes can crash into towers and mothers can die—will die—in your arms, but not yet, not yet. And in that cabin you are warm under an afghan on the couch crying and listening to Tom Waits on the stereo. And no one can shush you, tell you not to cry when you think how glad you are that you could do something—that *I* could do something—to stop my cat from hurting, and that he, that damn Rafiki could do his spirit guide animal thing for me, so selfless, dying for me. Making me stay and face it. Giving me a practice run.

We're nearly to Glen Arbor now, and a tourist has pulled in front of us on the highway. He slows way down at each cross street, hitting his blinker then turning it off, going—can it be?—even more slowly down the road. Our car doesn't like it slow, the rattle turns into a rumble again, and I'm back to my city driving self, cursing the other driver. Come on come on! Just make the goddamn turn! On the downhills I take my foot off the gas and it's not so bad, but when we start the slow rounding into a lakeside curve, something squeals under the hood.

"We're almost there. Come on," I say out loud to the car. "You can stop soon." The car in front turns finally, and I step on the gas, try to rev the engine up to a speed that it likes. Just a little further. Then we all can rest.

Philip, still in London, cried when I told him about the last trip to the vet over the phone, missing Rafiki, missing me.

"I'm coming back," he said, and maybe we both knew then he meant for good. And before we left Northern Michigan, we decided to marry. My mom lived long enough to be part of the wedding, and three months after that, I held her while she died.

When we reach Glen Arbor, we don't know where we are going. It's dusk now, but we guess at a turn, and then there's a sign for the place, and when we turn again, the motor stops, but the car doesn't. I crank the engine over and over—we're almost there, we're almost there—and it starts, and we limp the few yards and coast into the spot in front of this other cabin in the woods and we're here, we've made it.

It's nearly September again, and the leaves high in the trees are already starting their change. In the evening shadows, we unpack the car that is quiet now, no more rattle, no more ghost voices, and we leave it and go get some beers, some French fries, some whitefish.

At a table in a restaurant in the woods close to Lake Michigan, hundreds of miles from Chicago, two years from our last visit, we toast one another, the tenacious little car, the entire noisy, nostalgic trip. We don't say it out loud, but we toast, too, all that was lost. What is it about a place that draws you to it, no matter the trouble you've seen, no matter how sad you were the last time you were there? This is such a place, the place I escaped to when my mother got sick, where I could write in the quiet. The place where we drank coffee in a cool, dark kitchen the morning the towers went down, where we stood looking out at a great lake and agreed to spend our lives together, here, *here* here in the US, where we ran through the woods on a path that circled back to our cabin where Rafiki met us at the door, tail swishing and whiskers tickling our ankles. And we're so glad we made it; so damn glad to be here. Back in this place where we've been before. Back where some things ended, yes, but back where everything else started. 🪑

CONTRIBUTORS

CONTRIBUTOR BIOS

RANDALL ALBERS chairs the Fiction Writing Department at Columbia College Chicago and is Founding Producer of the Story Week Festival of Writers. His fiction and nonfiction have appeared in *Prairie Schooner*, *F Magazine*, *Writing in Education*, *Writer's Digest*, *TriQuarterly*, and elsewhere.

JC AEVALIOTIS is a Chicago-based writer and performer who holds a master's degree in religion and theater from Yale Divinity School. He has performed with various Second City-affiliated ensembles and several live-lit outfits in Chicago, and his writing has been seen in *Playboy* and heard on Chicago NPR affiliate WBEZ.

BOBBY BIEDRZYCKI is a writer, performer, and social activist. His writing has appeared in various publications and he has performed his stories at Steppenwolf Theatre, Goodman Theatre, and other venues throughout the United States. Bobby is an adjunct faculty member of the Fiction Writing Department at Columbia College Chicago and the Director of Programming for 2nd Story.

JULIA BORCHERTS is a co-founder of Reading Under the Influence and The Chicago Way literary series, a member of the 2nd Story collective, a fiction writing instructor at Columbia College Chicago, a theater columnist for *RedEye*, and a frequent contributor to *Time Out Chicago* and the *Windy City Times*.

CP CHANG, a company member of 2nd Story, is a writer and software consultant. He received his M.F.A. in fiction writing from Columbia College Chicago and was formerly an Associate Producer for Elephant Rock Productions. He is blessed to be married to Jessica Young, a teacher, performer, and writer.

AMANDA DELHEIMER DIMOND is a teacher, writer, and director, and has been 2nd Story's Artistic Director since 2007. She is an Artistic Associate of Adventure Stage Chicago, where she also teaches and directs. When she's not running 2nd Story, Amanda works in the Chicago public schools as a teaching artist.

MOLLY EACH is a Minnesota-born, Chicago-based writer, editor, and storyteller. Her fiction and creative nonfiction have been featured in *Fresh Yarn*, *Hair Trigger*, *Annalemma Quarterly*, *Eleven Eleven*, and on Chicago Public Radio. Check it all out at www.mollyeach.com.

BYRON FLITSCH is a writer living in Los Angeles and writes for *MTV*, *Forbes Travel*, and a variety of national publications. His creative nonfiction can be seen in *Toasted Cheese*, *Windy City Queer*, and more. He also founded *The Everyday Gay*, a publication about everyday gays doing exceptionally great things. Stalk him properly at www.byronflitsch.com.

KHANISHA FOSTER is a mixed-race actress, writer, teaching artist, the Associate Artistic Director of 2nd Story, an ensemble member of Teatro Vista, a 2009 TCG Young Leader of Color, and has collaborated with the Citizen's Theatre in Scotland. She is in the film *Chicago Boricua* and writing her memoir, *HEROIN(E)*.

JULIE GANEY is a Chicago-based writer/actor whose work has been featured on stages around the country, including solo shows developed out of 2nd Story: *The Half-Life of Magic* and *Love Thy Neighbor . . . Till It Hurts*. She is especially proud of her work as a teaching artist with students of all ages.

LOTT HILL is an activist, teacher, and storyteller living in Chicago with his husband and pit bull rescue pup. He regularly writes and performs with 2nd Story.

SARA KERASTAS is the Education Director and an Artistic Associate at About Face Theatre in Chicago. In 2010, she received a *Windy City Times* 30-Under-30 Award for leadership contributions to Chicago's LGBTQ community. She received her B.A. in English-Drama and Theatre and Women's Studies from McGill University in Montreal, Quebec.

LAWRENCE KERNS, M.D., is a writer and child psychiatrist who set out one summer to build a replica of Thoreau's cabin . . . with his four teenage kids . . . in his own backyard. "Foundationalysis" is an excerpt from his longer story, "Cabinalysis," currently being adapted as a stage play.

DEB R. LEWIS's work appears in the anthology *Windy City Queer*, plus many journals including *The Everyday Gay, Criminal Class Review, IsGreaterThan, Gertrude, Velvet Mafia,* and *Blithe House Quarterly.* Her unpublished novel, *Hades Son,* was a Project Queer Lit's Top-Three Finalist. She's won *Windy City Times' Pride Literary Supplement* Prose Prize. DebRLewis.com.

ERIC CHARLES MAY is an associate professor in the Fiction Writing Department at Columbia College Chicago and a former reporter for *The Washington Post.* His fiction has appeared in *Fish Stories* and *F* magazine. In addition to *Post* reporting, his nonfiction has appeared in *Sport Literate* and the *Chicago Tribune.*

PATRICIA ANN McNAIR is the author of *The Temple of Air,* a finalist for the Society of Midland Authors Best Book Award and Devil's Kitchen Reading Award. She's received four Illinois Arts Council Awards and was nominated for the Carnegie Foundation US Professor of the Year. McNair teaches in Columbia College Chicago's Fiction Writing Department.

Originally from Kent, Ohio, **MATT MILLER** is a Chicago-based stage director, teacher, and long-suffering Indians fan. His stories have been heard at The Moth (Story Slam Winner, February 2010), Essay Fiesta, Write Club, and 2nd Story, where he is an emeritus company member. Stalk him appropriately at www.mattmillerdirect.com.

KIM MORRIS is a writer, performer, storyteller, and editor. Check out Power Love for more: www.power-love.blogspot.com.

J. ADAMS OAKS is the author of the Booklist-starred novel *Why I Fight* (Simon and Schuster), a Junior Library Guild Selection included in ALA Best Books For Young Adults. His short work has appeared in numerous publications and anthologies and has been featured on WBEZ, Chicago Public Radio. Check it: www.jadamsoaks.com.

ANDREW REILLY is 2nd Story's Director of Publishing. His journalism, essays, photography, and fiction have appeared in a number of fine publications including *ALARM*, *The A.V. Club*, and *Norman Einstein's Sports & Rocket Science Quarterly*, among others. Visit him online at andrewreilly.org or in person in Chicago.

KIMBERLEE SOO is published by *INTHEFRAY*, *2D Magazine*, and *Cell Stories*. She has read for Featherproof, MCA's Literary Gangs of Chicago and Los Angeles's Mixed Roots Festival. Her acting credits include the Midwest premiere of David Henry Hwang's *Golden Child* for Silk Road Rising and projects with Goodman Theatre, Steppenwolf Theatre, About Face, and The Hypocrites.

MEGAN STIELSTRA is the author of *Everyone Remain Calm*, a story collection, and is the Literary Director for 2nd Story. Her writing appears in *Other Voices*, *Pank*, *Fresh Yarn*, *Pindeldyboz*, *Swink*, and *The Nervous Breakdown*, among others. She teaches creative writing and performance at Columbia College Chicago and The University of Chicago.

RIC WALKER is an actor, writer, director, improviser, and coach. He has performed in numerous plays, films, and countless improv shows. He has been a performer with many companies such as 2nd Story, ComedySportz, The Improvised Shakespeare Company, and The Second City. He is engaged in a struggle to find a truly delicious gluten-free pizza.

SAM WELLER's books include *The Bradbury Chronicles: The Life of Ray Bradbury* and *Listen to the Echoes: The Ray Bradbury Interviews*. Weller is also the co-editor of *Shadow Show: All-New Stories in Celebration of Ray Bradbury*, and an Associate Professor in the Fiction Writing Department at Columbia College Chicago.

BRIEFLY KNOCKED UNCONSCIOUS BY A LOW-FLYING DUCK

STORIES FROM 2ND STORY

ELEPHANT ROCK BOOKS

A Reader's Guide

Interview with Megan Stielstra.

In the spirit of 2nd Story's creative process, editors at Elephant Rock Books curated an interview with 2nd Story Literary Director Megan Stielstra about the collective, storytelling, Dreaming Big, and why a performance series wanted a book.

Elephant Rock Books: What is the origin of 2nd Story?

Megan Stielstra: In 2002, 2nd Story's founder, Adam Belcuore, put together a performance series on the second floor of Webster's Wine Bar, mostly friends telling stories over a glass of wine (or two or five). Those friends brought more friends, who brought more. After the first year, Adam hired our current Artistic Director, Amanda Delheimer Dimond, to direct. They both work in the Chicago theater community and brought in all sorts of amazing performers and sound designers, but felt they needed someone to help support the writing process, as well. Webster's is a pretty non-traditional theater space: imagine an L-shaped room, with tables and banquettes running around the perimeter and a bar at the far end. Wherever the storyteller is sitting, forty percent of the audience can't see them, so giving information through more performative techniques like gesture and facial expressions doesn't work. That information needs to be in the writing.

Adam saw me tell a story with a rock band at Subterranean and asked if I'd check out "this little thing" he produced at a wine bar. I was fascinated by how the oral telling and the written telling intersect, both in final product and within the creative process. 2nd Story was the perfect opportunity for me to delve into these ideas, learn from other artistic disciplines, and continue my work both as a writer and, now, a teacher of writing.

ERB: What experience had you had with oral storytelling?

MS: When I met Adam, I was in grad school and tending bar to put myself through. I'd spend my mornings studying literary craft and my evenings listening to these crazy, gut-wrenching stories from customers—people trying to connect, to amaze, to make it through another day. How were those stories told? How were they influenced by an immediate audience? What were the connections between *on the page* and *out loud*? You read Poe's "The Tell-Tale Heart," for example, and those words aren't just written there, static on paper. They are *screaming*. Kafka—*screaming*. Tolstoy, Bradbury, Marquez, Toni Morrison, Margaret Atwood, Dorothy Allison—screaming, whispering, right there across the table from you, hearts breaking in front of your eyes, telling you a story like you're the only person in the world.

ERB: We have the image of the writer, sitting alone at her desk creating; and then, theater companies, an ensemble of folks creating. How did you unite the two traditions?

MS: Adam introduced me to Amanda, and our challenge became just that, creating—and then facilitating—a collaborative process blending literary and theatrical traditions. We started with those Big Dream conversations, you know the ones, where you're all, "We'll totally buy a warehouse, and on the first floor we'll have a theatre; the second floor, a circus; and on the top we'll grow corn and make art—it'll be *awesome!*" That's how we talked, and it wasn't just the two of us; as time went by, more and more people brought their vision and time and expertise into our little family, which is why we've been able to actually pull off the crazy dreams of what 2nd Story could be: ". . . And we'll, like, do shows every month! And get DJs, and live musicians, and directors, and find people who have lived lives so profound and daring and thrilling that their stories must—*must!*—be shared! And we'll support them in that sharing with training in writing and performance, and we'll produce shows in all sorts of bars and theaters and festivals, and do conferences, and get grants, and teach outreach programs, and put out a print anthology—"

ERB: Glad you mentioned the "training in writing and performance." Can you describe the process of creating a show?

MS: We start brainstorming for our performances from that simple premise of sitting around with friends and telling stories. "You'll never believe what I saw today," we'll say, or, "What *that* makes me think of is *this*," or, "You think *that* was huge? *This* is huge!" We've done this with four people around a table, coming up with diverse responses to a similar theme, and we've done it with fifty people in the room, letting one story inspire the next, which then gives all sorts of ideas and permission and sometimes even a healthy kind of challenge to the other artists in the room. Say, someone shares a story that's totally insane or hilarious or confessional or furious about their childhood or family or survival or frustration. I'll think, "I have a story about that, too. Am I ready to share it?" Imagine one domino falling and setting off a hundred others, or how, when popcorn is on the fire, it starts with one kernel popping and then tons more explode.

ERB: Can you give an example where that process produced a story that was performed? Or better yet, performed and in this anthology?

MS: Khanisha Foster's story "The Kids and The King" was written for a show at Open Books around the theme of literacy. We put four very different storytellers around a table with a curator, and we all swapped stories, digging into the question of what literacy really means. You can think about it in terms of words and writing, but there's also visual literacy, musical literacy, cultural literacy. Khanisha is a teaching artist, and wanted to explore what she'd learned from one particular student, Andre. I remember the other people at the table, myself included, lighting up as she told us about him. You can really *see* what listening looks like: we were all leaning forward, totally engaged, waiting for the shoe to drop, gasping aloud. That's when you really know you've got something: when you can feel the story through the audience, be the audience four or four hundred.

Once we knew the story Khanisha would be telling, we encouraged the other three to think as widely as possible about experiences they'd like to share, so we could have as diverse an evening as possible. Diversity is a huge part of our mission: diversity of experience, of storyteller, of tone and structure and voice. If you want the human experience, you have to hear from as many voices as possible, all covering their lives from different ages and lessons and points of understandings, different passions and mistakes and life choices. We're not going to produce a show exploring technology and have four stories from four guys about four XBOXes. We'll have one XBOX, a woman from NASA, a crazy online dating story, and a vibrator expert.

After all four storytellers have decided on subject matter, they then go home and get those ideas down on the page. From there, they're in development with curators for a month or so, getting together to share drafts and to give-and-take feedback. Then, about a month before the final performance, the group meets again at what we call a Passing the Torch meeting, where the curator passes the work onto a director to help get the work off the page. Finally, the storytellers work with sound designers, DJ's or live bands.

All of this collaboration informs the writing process in really fascinating ways, and one of the most exciting things for me about working with 2nd Story is how it's informed how I teach writing.

ERB: Since you mentioned teaching, can you speak a bit about 2nd Story's educational programming?

MS: Many members of 2nd Story's company and staff—and several of the storytellers, directors, and designers with whom we collaborate—are teachers. Supporting people in the telling of their own stories is part of the mission of our organization, and offering training in literary and performative skills is integral to the art we make and how we make it. Plus—and this is super-important—we have *fun*.

We run workshops through our own in-house training program, and also partner with different community and educational organizations at both the K-12 and University level. Our teaching artists work in the public schools in residencies and after school programming, run the summer high school intensive program at Goodman Theatre, and teach college-level classes in both creative writing and theater. Most of this work currently happens in Chicago, our home-base, and in Los Angeles, where 2nd Story has recently sprouted wings. We also travel to facilitate workshops in both oral and written storytelling.

Anyone interested in our outreach should drop us an email through our website, or, better yet, let's meet for coffee.

ERB: So after ten years of performing and educating, why would a performance series produce a print anthology?

MS: In high school, I was the kind of geek who cut class in order to go to the library. Tolkien, Shakespeare, Steinbeck—but what really rocked my world was Richard Wright's *Black Boy*. There's a scene where the character of Richard gets a library card for the first time and suddenly, reading novels, he's able to understand people that are different than himself. Wright wrote, "It was a feeling of something new, of being affected by something that made the look of the world different." In that moment, the world opened up for me. We were, on some level, sharing an experience. Picture it: this sheltered, small-town girl in Southeast Michigan connecting with an adult man in the Jim Crow South. It changed the way I looked at history, showed me a part of the world I'd never imagined, challenged me to examine aspects of myself I didn't know were there.

ERB: That's the power of literature.

MS: That day in the library was a gift. That book was a gift.

ERB: It is your hope this anthology will affect readers' view of their world?

MS: For me—and for many of us at 2nd Story who came to our love of stories through reading—this anthology is an opportunity to share experiences with a wider audience. Every story in these pages has been performed live, some of them multiple times, and whether it's for twenty people in a bookstore, eighty in a wine bar, three hundred in a rock club, or five hundred at the Goodman, you can always feel the connection between teller and audience; the laughter, the gasps, the tenor of the silence. I believe that our reading audience will experience those connections, too; that the stories in this book stand on the page just as strongly as they do in performance. Long before they ever made it onstage, these stories went through the hands of the curators, editors, and directors on 2nd Story's Story Development Team. Sometimes, those hands were mine, and I remember sitting alone, reading those pages: the laughter, gasping, and terrifying silence.

ERB: Can you give us an example of a story that made you laugh, gasp or soil your britches?

MS: I can go on and on about how reading all these stories affected me: Kimberlee Soo's "CoverGirl" made me think about how harsly we compare ourselves to others. Sam Weller's "Amber" made me remember all the times my fantasies didn't translate into reality. I still cry when I read Ric Walker's "Push, Kick, Coast." Randy Albers' "Here Comes Trouble" reminds me that no matter how hard it gets, we still have to live, madly and completely. Lott Hill's "Crazy For You" made me consider the moment my own morality has been tested. After reading Deb R. Lewis's "Why I Hate Strawberries," I wanted to set the entire world on fire, and then, in the same breath, save it forever, and the title story of this book, "Briefly Knocked Unconscious By a Low-Flying Duck," made me cry in one paragraph and, in the next, pee my pants laughing.

The sheltered, small-town girl I once was is *horrified* that I told you about peeing my pants. But also? That same small-town girl?—she'd never have seen one of 2nd Story's live shows, or any live show. Too far to travel, too expensive, too edgy. But maybe now, in a Southeast Michigan library, she'll find herself in one our stories. She'll be affected by something that makes the world look different. And hopefully, if we've done our job right, she'll be inspired to tell her own.

ERB: After ten years of performances you have banked quite an archive. How were the essays selected for the anthology?

MS: Currently, 2nd Story performs three or four shows per month, constantly curating new material with new storytellers. So yes, our ten-year-old archive is vast. We work with amazing people who've led amazing lives, and write about their experiences with wit and grace and bravery. The sheer volume of stories they've told—the sheer volume of stories 2nd Story has produced—completely blew my mind. Choosing the twenty-three that live within these pages was . . . this might sound overdramatic, but it was *painful.*

ERB: Why painful?

MS: There are so many!

ERB: And after the pain subsided?

MS: More pain because new stories are happening all the time. And we haven't heard yours yet!

ERB: Okay, so after you took a couple Advil?

MS: We got to work. 2nd Story has teams for all sorts of different projects (like our super-swanky new website! You should totally come visit us there!), and about a year ago, we started a Publishing Committee with the intent of finding and creating ways for our stories to live after they've been performed. Translation: eight smart, excited, and slightly crazy people getting together in our Director Andrew's living room to drink beer and Dream Big. We talk about our podcast series, so our stories can come into *your* living room; our blog, *In the Chair,* that documents our work and the kickass people we work with; using social media for interactive storytelling with our audience; literary journals and magazines and, now, this book.

In thinking about what stories we wanted to include, we started by talking to people: our company, staff and board; storytellers, directors and designers; audience members who've been with us for years. "What stories are still sticking in your heads?" we asked. As you might imagine, that was a very long list, including stories from our most recent season, such as JC Aevaliotis's "Hollyweird," all the way back to ones we produced nearly ten years ago, like the title story. That list served as a jumping-off point to curate this anthology, which we did the same way we curate performances: aiming for as much diversity as possible, both insofar as the identity and life experience of our storytellers—age, gender, race, sexual orientation—and the way the stories are crafted—voice, structure, vantage point, tone.

ERB: Still, after ten years and umpteen performances, that sounds like a long list.

MS: It was mammoth. So, imagine Post-It notes covering the wall of our studio, each with a story title and multiple labels depending on subject matter and tone: *This story is sad; this story is hilarious. The narrator is thirteen; the narrator is forty. Parenting from the point of view of the parent; parenting from the point of view of the kid. Someone dies in this story. Drugs in this story. Sex in this story. Identity. Faith. Loss.* It was a giant, messy, wonderful puzzle. Eventually, someone was smart enough to put all these notes and discussions into a spreadsheet, and we narrowed down the list with more questions: do these stories stand on the page as strongly as they do in performance? Are the elements of tone, pacing, pauses, gestures, facial expression, and music translating into the literary craft? Some of the stories in this anthology went through another round of rewrites to make sure that was the case.

ERB: And this is where we got involved in the process: translating from stage to page.

MS: In our performances, we always rely on a final outside eye—the director—to make sure the stories are cohesive. In the case of this anthology, our publisher at Elephant Rock Books, Jotham Burrello, served that role, and we're beyond grateful for the care he gave these stories. So many of us involved in this project have seen these stories performed a hundred times, and it's difficult to be totally objective with the words on the page when you've been hearing them aloud for years. For example, Jotham might say, "What is the tone you're going for here?" and I'd be all, "How can you not know that? Obviously, it's—" and then I'd look at the page and see it wasn't there. It was there in the performance. So then we'd go back to the writer and say, "You know how in your performance of this piece, you kind of yell this line? That needs to be in the writing. Let's talk about how to do that." We do this same sort of thing in the college writing classes I teach. "How does reading the work out loud inform the writing process? How does performance translate to the page? If you're stuck in the writing, can telling it aloud help you break through?"

When we were done with that selection and editing process, we settled on twenty-three stories. I think we were able to preserve our goal of to feature stories that represent as much diversity as possible: diversity of storyteller, experience, story structure, tone, style, and voice.

ERB: What are your expectations for the book? Or in 2nd Story speak, the Big Dreams?

MS: Our dream for this book is to further 2nd Story's belief that sharing stories has the power to educate, connect, and inspire. Every day, we tell stories: to our parents or co-workers or partners or friends. We tell them on first dates, to get jobs, to win votes, to educate and connect and inspire. 2nd Story exists to host the sharing of those stories—the book you're holding now in your hands is an integral part of that. The book you're holding now in your hands is an integral part of that. We hope it will make you laugh, and maybe cry, and maybe push you to set the entire world on fire, and then, in the same breath, save it forever.

ERB: You dream big.

MS: Is there any other way?

ERB: Any more you'd like to add?

MS: Above all else, we hope the stories in this book will inspire you to tell your own. Pour yourself some coffee, or a glass of wine (or two or five). Meet your friends at a rock club, join some people for dinner, call up your mom or dad. "I just read this crazy thing," you can say. "And it made me think about that one time I . . . " *What? That one time you what?*

If the stories in this book are the first stories, yours are the second stories. We'd love to hear them.

Questions for Discussion

1) If you were choosing three or four stories to be performed together for an audience, which stories would you select? Are there any connections you see insofar as theme? Is there a particular order you'd put them in? Any special reason for your choices?

2) At 2nd Story, we spend a lot of time talking about what happens in a story versus what it's about. Are there any stories that seem to be about more than one thing?

3) Consider each one of these stories to be a "first story." The "second" story is yours: what experiences from your own life come after reading? For example, in Ric Walker's "Push, Kick, Coast," the narrator experiences the death of a friend. Do you have a story about the first time you experienced a great loss?

4) Some stories are about heavy, serious topics but have sections told in a lighter tone. Where do you find shifts in tone in a given story? How do you imagine it would sound if you heard it out loud? (Read aloud with your group to experience it.)

5) Some of the stories in this collection are in past tense; some, like Kimberlee Soo's story "CoverGirl," are in present tense. How does the tense affect your experience of a story?

6) These stories were originally written for performance. Where do you feel the storyteller speaking directly to you? What literary techniques translate an oral telling to a written telling?

7) Narrative distance has to do with how far in time the storyteller is from the events in the story. How does this distance, or in some cases, lack of distance, affect the lens through which it is told? Are there moments in the story where you feel the distance changes? How would the story be different if it was told closer or further from the events?

Additional Resources for Educators:

We hope you'll consider the book in your hand not only a collection of great stories, but also a teaching tool.

Integral to 2nd Story's mission is the idea that every one of our stories is a jumping-off point—an invitation to the reader (or listener) to then tell his or her own story about a lie that got out of hand, or a summer where everything changed, or the experience of losing a friend. That's what our name, 2nd Story, refers to: We'll tell you the first story, then you'll tell someone the story that it brings to mind— the second story.

If you're interested in writing your own 2nd Story-style piece, or if you're an educator interested in helping your students create stories of their own, we have extensive information on our website that can assist you in that endeavor. You'll find brainstorming exercises, structure ideas and editing tips that we use in our work every day, in addition to information on our collaborative process, and how we actually work together to create these intimate stories.

Here are some ideas to get you pointed in the right direction:

1) We always start our process with brainstorming, using exercises that get us thinking about events in our lives—large or small—that somehow changed the way we see things. We use questions like, "Think of a moment in your life when your view of the world changed." "Think of a time you left something behind—maybe a habit, a person, or an idea." "Think of a time you failed miserably (or succeeded triumphantly)." We urge writers in this form to start with an event, rather than "I want to write about my Dad."

2) Narrative distance—how far the teller is from the events in the story—is important when approaching those stories; in other words, if there is enough distance between the teller and the event for the story to be told in a meaningful way. Educators can help students determine whether they are ready to delve into certain stories and whether the teller is a safe enough distance from certain events to actually make create meaning from them, for themselves and for an audience.

3) Once we find a compelling moment to write about, we go right to that moment of the story and start writing. Our stories are based in scene, with people in a particular place speaking to each other through dialogue. The most important moments in our stories tend to happen in scene, and often starting right there seems to help us achieve the intimate feeling we're looking for. Then we fill in the before and after.

4) Our stories are all first person narrative, meaning that the teller is the protagonist, the character we care about most.

A 2nd Story piece might be centered around the day your Mom finally stood up to your Dad in the kitchen when you were fourteen, but it needs to be about *you*—how it affected *your* life or the way *you* saw things.

5) Because our work is meant to be shared, a sense of audience is vital to our writing process. Questions like "Why am I telling this story now?" "Why should anyone besides your family and friends care about this story?" and, "What's universal in this piece?" are considered as we wrestle not only *with what happens in a story*—the events, or narrative—but also *what the story is about*, and why it would have meaning for someone else.

6) Since we have time constraints within our shows and because we share our stories out loud, our editing process is rigorous. We read our drafts to each other over and over, utilizing many of teacher and choreographer Liz Lerman's critical response techniques, collaborating and working together to help the writer hone the story until it is ready for a director and performance.

But this is just a sketch of our process! Visit our website, www.2ndstory. com, and you'll find a myriad of specific tools and exercises that will support your work in the teaching of writing and performance.

ACKNOWLEDGEMENTS

We're forever indebted to Jotham Burrello, who believed our work could live on the page as much as it lives in performance.

Thank you to Amanda Schwarz, Lee Nagan, and Dan Prazer from Fisheye Graphic Services for making this book so unbelievably pretty.

This anthology was partially funded via Kickstarter, and though the list of kind and generous donors is too long to enumerate here, you know who you are. Thank you for your faith in us. We wouldn't have made it ten feet without you. We're also grateful to Alex Bonner and Bailout Pictures for the awesome video.

2nd Story is a collective of story-makers and story-lovers working to build community through the power of storytelling, and we're grateful to all of our collaborators for the many, many ways they've touched this book, including (but certainly not limited to): our Publishing Committee, for working their butts off to make this thing happen; our company, board, staff, and interns for their late nights, hard work, and lofty vision; our storytellers, curators, directors, producers, and designers, who've influenced these stories in countless ways; and to Adam Belcuore who, so many years ago, started 2nd Story on the second floor of Webster's Wine Bar. In your wildest dreams, did you ever imagine you'd be holding this book in your hands?

We also want to acknowledge our friends, spouses, partners, roommates, moms and dads (and on and on) who listened to countless drafts, came to a ton of events, and lent us their ears and hearts and sometimes cars, all in the pursuit of great storytelling. Thank you so much.

Finally, for our audience: you are the reason for everything we do.